MW00529754

Vanity Faith

Searching for Spirituality among the Stars

Terrance W. Klein

LITURGICAL PRESS
Collegeville, Minnesota

www.litpress.org

Excerpt from William Frye, "The Wizard of Roz," *Vanity Fair* 500 (April 2002). Used by permission of William Frye.

Excerpt from Stefan Kanfer, *Ball of Fire: The Tumultuous Life and Comic Art of Lucille Ball*, copyright © 2003 by Stefan Kanfer. Used by permission of Alfred A. Knopf, a division of Random House, Inc.

Excerpt from Frank DiGiacomo, "A Rock of Her Own," *Vanity Fair* 552 (August 2006). Used by permission of Frank DiGiacomo.

Excerpts from Robert Gottlieb, "DAH-LING: The Strange Case of Tallulah Bankhead," *New Yorker* (May 16, 2005). Used by permission of Robert Gottlieb.

Excerpt from *The Ballad of Gilligan's Isle*. Words and music by Sherwood Schwartz and George Wyle. © 1964, 1966 (copyrights renewed) EMI U Catalog, Inc. All rights controlled by EMI U Catalog, Inc. (Publishing) and Alfred Publishing Co., Inc. (Print). All rights reserved. Used by permission of Alfred Publishing.

Scripture texts in this work are taken from the *New Revised Standard Version Bible: Catholic Edition* © 1989, 1993, Division of Christian Education of the National Council of the Churches of Christ in the United States of America. Used by permission. All rights reserved.

Cover design by Ann Blattner.

© 2009 by Order of Saint Benedict, Collegeville, Minnesota. All rights reserved. No part of this book may be reproduced in any form, by print, microfilm, microfiche, mechanical recording, photocopying, translation, or by any other means, known or yet unknown, for any purpose except brief quotations in reviews, without the previous written permission of Liturgical Press, Saint John's Abbey, PO Box 7500, Collegeville, Minnesota 56321-7500. Printed in the United States of America.

1	2	3	4	5	6	7	8	9

Library of Congress Cataloging-in-Publication Data

Klein, Terrance W., 1958–
      Vanity faith : searching for spirituality among the stars / Terrance W. Klein.
         p. cm.
      Includes bibliographical references.
      ISBN 978-0-8146-3220-8 (pbk.)
      1. Spirituality—Catholic Church.   2. Popular culture—Religious aspects—Christianity.   3. Motion pictures—Religious aspects—Christianity.
4. Motion picture actors and actresses.   5. Television actors and actresses.
I. Title.

   BX2350.65.K59 2009
   261.5'2—dc22   2008040181

For Mom
the biggest star I know

Well, actually, the only one

Contents

Preview

The Far West Side

Today, when other New Yorkers ask me where I grew up, I say, "the Far West Side." And that works, because to them that means: it's a bit of a walk from there to Broadway. Is it ever! I grew up on the very far west side, Kansas, and while I was growing up amid those golden wheat fields, I realized something important. I realized that most people were *not* growing up in Kansas. In fact, every time I turned on the television or went to the movies, people seemed to be growing up everywhere but Kansas! Buffy and Jody, and of course Sissy, lived in New York with their Uncle Bill on *Family Affair*. *The Courtship of Eddie's Father* was taking place in California, while Will Robinson was growing up in outer space of all places, hopefully on his way, with the Space Family Robinson, to a planet called Alpha Centari.

Just about everything was happening someplace other than Kansas, either on one of the coasts or in another galaxy. And looking at it from the Jayhawker State, it all seemed to amount to pretty much the same thing: I had been born in the wrong place. Granted, Dorothy Gale had been born in Kansas, but what consolation was that? She also wanted to be on the other side of the rainbow ASAP.

So I made a resolution. When I grew up, I would journey to the place where Patty Lane's cousin Kathy had come from on *The Patty*

Duke Show. I loved her accent, and I wanted to marry a girl who talked like that. At the time I didn't identify it as an English accent. I just knew that no one in Kansas spoke that way. I also knew that Kathy "had been most everywhere, from Zanzibar to Barclay Square," but that "Patty had only seen the sights a girl can see from Brooklyn Heights."[1] I wasn't all that sure where Brooklyn Heights was, but if the girls there talked like Kathy, I knew I'd one day be joining them.

Have you ever tried to recapture the image of a place you once carried, the one you had before you got there? Radio City Music Hall, perhaps? Strange thing about those early images. In our imagination, we paint them of longed-for places. They nourish our dreams. But when we actually arrive at our once-dreamt location, our homemade images are replaced by real ones of the place itself. Then it's difficult even to recall how we once pictured the place. There's something sad in losing the homespun images of the heart, even if it's a natural part of pursuing our dreams.

So here's a question. Who hasn't imagined heaven, thought of what it would be like, tried to picture the other side of the rainbow? Obviously something comes to mind when we say the word "heaven," and, unless we're very simple folk, it's probably not clouds and wings. But then what is it? What do you picture?

In the book of Revelation, the last book in the New Testament, St. John presents a fascinating vision of a great multitude of people in white robes holding palm branches and surrounding Jesus, whom John identifies as the Lamb of God (7:9-17). Where did the vision come from? Scholars offer an interesting hypothesis. Whatever spiritual or psychic event might have occurred in the life of John the Seer, his vision of the heavenly court is probably modeled upon very early Christian liturgy: the elders, the incense, the throne, and the lamb upon the altar. In other words, Christian worship wasn't designed to imitate John's writings. Just the opposite. The writings were probably drawn from liturgical experience. When John pictured heaven, what came to mind was the church at prayer.

The *Universal Catechism of the Catholic Church* offers an interesting description of heaven, one very closely linked to the words of Jesus in the Gospel of John: "My sheep hear my voice; I know them, and they follow me. I give them eternal life, and they will never perish" (10:27). The catechism says: "Heaven is the ultimate end and fulfillment of the deepest human longings, the state of supreme, definitive happiness. To live in heaven is 'to be with Christ.'"[2]

Notice that instead of a place, somewhere over the rainbow, the catechism speaks of a relationship. We do something similar when we say that being with another is heaven, or its opposite! Do you remember that rascal Jean-Paul Sartre saying in his play *No Exit* that "hell is other people"?[3] Either way, it's relationships that tend to make wherever we are a heaven or a hell.

This little book is about the stage and screen (and, for that matter, the off-stage, off-camera) relationships of the stars, many of whom began their lives in zip codes far from Hollywood or the Great White Way. Who knows? Some of these stars may well be saints today. My church tends to name a lot of saints, though so far Audrey Hepburn and Coco Chanel have both been ignored. (What's up with that?)

My point is, who says Christian spirituality has to be stuffy? I have been in love with God and the movies and television since I began my showbiz career in Ellinwood, Kansas, where I distributed flyers for the local movie theater in exchange for free admission, saving a quarter per show! Everything you need to know about grace you can learn from watching Audrey Hepburn movies, and you can learn a lot about the soul by simply paying attention to your own desires. Falling in love? The stars wrote the script. Suffering? They've been there before you and found the strength to survive. God may be the world's oldest mystery, but hints of whom God is, where God is to be found, and what God might want of us abound in biographies of the stars and in the movies and sitcoms we've come to love.

And speaking of stars, besides Mom, the biggest star I know, I should mention the people of Park Slope, Brooklyn, who listened to these ruminations from the pew with indulgence, and also Hans Christoffersen and Susan Sink, editors at Liturgical Press. Hans guided the manuscript through development while Susan acted as an infusion of grace itself with editorial comments, asking me about what I was really trying to say. Answering her questions has made for much better writing on my part.

Am I making saints out of stars? No, I know that many of them made moral mistakes that shouldn't be envied or emulated, but the thought behind these pages is that we can learn from the lives of others. God tends to reveal God's self in the web of relationships that we call lovers, family, and friends. Reading the life-scripts of others may help us to recognize our own cues. And maybe pondering life among the stars can set your gaze even a bit higher than Alpha Centari.

So, go ahead and use your imagination. In the end, it won't prove up to the task of picturing heaven. The truth behind the word "heaven" is simply our eternal, joyfully fulfilled life with God. Will heaven be more like California, Brooklyn Heights, or outer space? Will the women there talk like Kathy? I don't know, but something tells me that on the other side of the rainbow I'll still see those beautiful Kansas wheat fields, the ones I never gave much notice as a child.

1

The Soul

Hearing the Casting Call

The Rockette Experience

My friend Patti called from Ohio. "Guess what Steve is giving me for the big day?"

"What big day?"

"My fiftieth birthday! How can you ask what big day?" I've forgotten to mention that Patti, a very attractive woman, has (perhaps) not fully made peace with aging. I guess we're on the same page there.

"I don't know, Patti. What is Steve giving you?"

"What have I always wanted to be ever since I was a little girl?"

"Mrs. Paul McCartney, but I can't imagine your husband arranging that."

"Besides that—even before Paul McCartney. I've always wanted to be a Rockette, and Steve found a program called 'The Rockette Experience.' I get to be a Rockette for a day!"

"So you're coming to New York to be a Rockette?"

"I am. But Steve can't get away that weekend, and that's where you come in." If you knew Patti the way I know Patti you'd realize that this is like Fred Mertz being told he has to go onstage for the long-suffering Ricky Ricardo.

"You see, the program is primarily designed for young girls, but I've checked. They said that since I've been taking dance lessons—like, forever—I would be welcome. It's just that the others will be considerably younger, and will bring along a parent, and—you know my mother—she can't possibly make the trip. That's where you come in."

And so come December, I dressed myself as paternally as possible, going for the Fred MacMurray look in *My Three Sons,* and took my girl off to be a Rockette for a day. I wasn't the only father there. Granted, I was the only one of my kind of father. For the most part, the other parents were moms. Besides being paternal, my job was to videotape the day for all the folks back in Columbus.

I was happy to see that there were other women participating along with Patti: several college girls, one of whom had recently had a baby; a nurse; and another woman who had to be close to Patti's age. They danced and smiled, and smiled and danced their way through ballet, tap, and dramatic routines. "A Rockette always smiles!" they were told. Usually I didn't understand the dance instructions the Rockettes gave, and I had little idea of whether they were being well-executed by the Rockettes-for-a-day. I just smiled, figuring that's what a Rockette's dad should do as well, and I volunteered to take pictures for others. For much of the day I was holding five cameras.

Of course my cameras couldn't capture what was in that room. It was filled with dreams. Little girls and their mothers dreaming of a future stage. Older women dreaming of a turn not taken. Young, beautiful Rockettes living their dream. My cameras could only catch the smiles, not the dreams.

The prophet Isaiah was a dreamer. He spoke of a glorious servant of the Lord who would be a light to the nations. John the Baptist was told that he would recognize the Savior, because he would see the Spirit rest upon him. But all that is ancient history. John's discernment is finished. Ours has just begun. The question is, how do we recognize the Spirit of God? How do we know what God wants, or where God is active? If we didn't become a Rockette,

2

did we take a wrong turn in the dance? Or is the abiding, deep desire to be a Rockette an important clue about the stage God sets for our performance, even if that performance isn't in Radio City Music Hall?

No one wrote more lucidly on that question than St. Ignatius of Loyola. His *Spiritual Exercises,* written in the sixteenth century, deal with the discernment of spirits: how we know God's will. It's hard to say yes if you can't figure out what God wants. A simple, but nonetheless true, entrance to this rule is to note that good people should pay attention to their hearts, which is to say their emotions. Here is one of Ignatius' fundamental rules for the discernment of spirits:

> In the case of persons who are earnestly purging away their sins, and who are progressing from good to better in the service of God our Lord . . . it is characteristic of the evil spirit to cause gnawing anxiety, to sadden, and to set up obstacles. In this way he unsettles them by false reasons aimed at preventing their progress.
>
> But with persons of this type it is characteristic of the good spirit to stir up courage and strength, consolations, tears, inspirations, and tranquility. He makes things easier and eliminates all obstacles, so that the persons may move forward in doing good.[1]

As Ignatius sees it, we shouldn't allow negative emotions to deter us from the good, and we need to listen carefully to the positive emotions we receive. If the thought of dancing makes you want to dance, maybe that's because God made you a dancer. So, why aren't you on the boards?

If God made us, if God put deep desires into our hearts, isn't the first task of responding to God's will simply to recognize our own deepest desires and to act upon them? I spent so many years in seminary trying to figure out what God wanted, but there was never a day I didn't want to be a teacher. Isn't God clever, hiding the divine will in the last place I'd look, my heart?

Paul begins his first letter to the Corinthians with a simple self-identification: "Paul, called to be an apostle of Christ Jesus by the will of God" (1:1). We think he had it easy. We'd know what to do if we were knocked to the ground, but Paul would never have been on that road to Damascus without following where his heart led, a heart in love with his Jewish faith. Why do we expect the Lord to show us the second step when we so often refuse the first?

Those who know my friend Patti well know not to let her sit and drink at bar counters. She has a tendency to get up and do Irish jigs on top of them. Steve and I turn red. Patti only hears the music, but to hear the music of the heart and to dance is surely akin to the wild, divine inspiration with which the Spirit of God first fashioned our world.

Getting It Right

I like to think of myself as a careful learner, but I offer the following confession of "things I got wrong." My mistakes started early. For example, my mother is a strong believer in after-lunch naps for children. As a child I would have made Goldilocks proud of the way I took to the practice, but I didn't get the name quite right. I'd grab my blanket and say, "Come on, Mama, let's *belax*."

I also messed up on Superman. I was a very early fan. We're talking George Reeves, not the current denizens of *Smallville*. Every afternoon our television set would boom: "The Adventures of Superman. Faster than a speeding bullet! More powerful than a locomotive! Able to leap tall buildings at a single bound! 'Look, up in the sky! It's a bird! It's a plane! It's Superman!'" And the announcer would say, "Yes, it's Superman, strange visitor from another planet who came to Earth with powers and abilities far beyond those of mortal men. Superman, who can change the course of mighty rivers, bend steel in his bare hands; and who, disguised as Clark Kent, mild-mannered reporter for a great metropolitan newspaper, fights a never ending battle for truth, justice, and the American way."[2] That's what I wanted to do, fight that never-ending battle, right there in Kansas.

But there was a scientific miscalculation on my part. In kindergarten I thought Superman's flying abilities came from simply wearing his cape. I didn't realize that in order to fly one has to be born under the red sun of Krypton with its much denser gravitational field. Fortunately when I received a Sears Roebuck Superman suit for Christmas that year, my mother coaxed me off the roof before my speculations proved calamitous.

Sadly my theological insights have likewise been checkered. For the longest time I thought God was the point above the sanctuary of our Kansas church where the neo-Gothic arches met, because that's where the priest always looked when he prayed.

Or take first grade, when Father Bahr gave us a small talk on the process of becoming a priest. I followed him avidly until someone asked him about studies. He said that priests spend eight to twelve years in the "*cemetery*"! That's what I heard, and I couldn't picture myself sitting on a cold tombstone with a book for eight years. Wouldn't that cause piles?

This little book about movies, television shows, and the stars who made them is also a book about spirituality, with lots of theology thrown in, because I believe that theology fosters good spirituality, at least it does if it's good theology. I like to define theology as the lifetime of study one does to recuperate from catechesis, the stuff we were taught as children about God. And I'm not bashing the priests, laity, and religious sisters who taught me about the faith. I'm bashing the notion that what we learned as children should be set in stone. That sort of thinking causes intellectual piles!

Knowledge is both an uphill climb and a slippery slope. For example, any scientist who knows the craft also knows that science itself can never provide an absolute, irreformable fact. This is because every scientific answer depends upon the field of inquiry that prompted the question. It's always open to revision on the basis of further evidence or the development of a new explanatory theory. In fact, every new scientific insight subtly rearranges the value of every previous insight, just as the significance of a single chess piece alters with each move in the game.

So why is it that so many of us still believe that every religious truth we've ever learned must be either absolutely unchanging, exactly the way we learned it in primary school, or somehow quite false? That's not much of an option, and if it were true it would make religious knowledge unlike any other sort of human knowing: either unchanging or untrue. I'll take a pass on both those choices for the simple reason that our knowledge changes as we change and grow, adapt, and mature.

By definition, God is unchanging, but our *ideas* about God constantly change. God is not an object we've caught in the butterfly net that we call the human mind. This is why a medieval church council, the Fourth Lateran, could insist that "between Creator and creature no similarity can be expressed without implying an even greater dissimilarity."[3] So what comes into our minds when we say that God is merciful, or just, or beautiful, is still so much less than what God really is.

Echoing a long tradition in the church, St. Thomas Aquinas taught that "since God infinitely exceeds the power of our intellect, any form we conceive cannot completely represent the divine essence, but merely has, in some small measure, an imitation of it."[4] I mean this when I tell people, if you can picture it, it ain't God. All of our pictures, images, and notions of God fall short of God.

When the theological acumen of his disciples led to quarrels (talk about getting things wrong!), Jesus placed a child in their midst and told them to welcome the child (Mark 9:36-37). What does it mean to welcome the child into the world of faith? Doesn't it have something to do with adopting the attitude of a child, believing that the world is still an open book, one well worth rereading, still a place of wonder and discovery?

Religion asks ultimate questions. It doesn't offer ultimate answers, not if by ultimate one means answers that stop all further questions. Every answer our faith offers is always an invitation to probe, to explore, to deepen. A giant among American theologians, Paul Tillich, once wrote:

> The condition of man's relation to God is first of all one of *not* having, *not* seeking, *not* knowing, and *not* grasping. A religion in which

that is forgotten, no matter how ecstatic or active or reasonable, replaces God by its own creation of an image of God. . . . It is not easy to endure this not having God, this waiting for God. . . . For how can God be possessed? Is God a thing that can be grasped and known among other things? Is God less than a human person? We always have to wait for a human being. Even in the most intimate communion among human beings, there is an element of *not* having and *not* knowing, and of waiting. Therefore, since God is infinitely hidden, free, and incalculable, we must wait for Him in the most absolute and radical way. He is God for us just in so far as we do *not* possess Him. . . . We have God through *not* having Him.[5]

Those words may not be comforting in a modern world of uncertainty, but faith is a journey *into* knowing, not a book of dusty truths. In love, God does give God's self to us, and, even if it is not the final word, faith is a real knowing, not just speculation. Faith is *our* way of knowing. It is not the last word. It never can be, because that word belongs to God alone.

So put aside the crusty surety of adulthood and welcome the child of faith and wonder. And don't jump off the roof any time soon, even with a really good cape!

Herro, Who Calling Please?

One of my favorite actresses was remembered several years ago in a *Vanity Fair* profile. All right, fine! A dirty little secret is now out in the open. I sometimes read articles in *Vanity Fair*. I'm not proud of the admission. Confessing that one peruses *Vanity Fair* is akin to admitting to a subscription to *Playboy,* except that with *Playboy* you swear that you only read the articles and never look at the pictures. With *Vanity Fair* it's just the opposite.

But I loved Rosalind Russell in *Auntie Mame,* and I consider *The Trouble with Angels* the greatest movie ever made. Go figure! So I was drawn to the memoir of her long-time associate, producer, and friend, William Frye.

Frye writes:

Some Beverly Hills women I know are harder to reach than the Pope. Not Roz. She often answered her own phone, but she usually did it with a fake Oriental accent: "Herro, Brisson residence. Who calling, please?" If she wasn't in the mood to talk, she'd say, "Missy no here. Call back."

I would interrupt her and say, "Roz, dear, it's Bill." And she'd say, "Oh, hi, sweetheart. How are you?"

One day Irene Dunne asked me, "Why does Roz use that Japanese accent when she answers the phone?"

I said, "I suppose she wants to find out who's calling before she talks to them. I just call her on it. Don't you?"

"Oh, no," said Irene. "I would never spoil her game. She just loves play-actressing."[6]

Were I an actor of her stature and living in a world before voice mail, I might do the same. Why? Because I find myself trying similar tactics with God. God often sounds like a ringing phone, and I don't know what to do with that except try to duck, like Doubting Thomas. Now there's a thesis. God sounds like a ringing phone? What do I mean by that? Give me a few paragraphs, and I'll try to work it through.

Whatever else a ringing phone does, it always summons us into the future. And don't we have the tiniest emotional twinge every time it rings? Maybe it's someone on the line from whom I'd love to hear. Maybe he or she is coming to see me. Maybe we'll go to the Plaza and have high tea, and I'll hear something so wonderfully life changing that I'll never regret having answered that phone.

Of course, maybe it's a telemarketer surging up from hell. Maybe the credit card company is calling to ask about charges I've never made. And isn't there always someone whom you're hoping will never call again?

A ringing telephone has all the wonderful ambiguity of the future: could be cool, could be crap. Who knows? But, one way or another, we're constantly summoned into the future, and it's a future that always remains outside our control, no matter how much insurance we buy or how many contingency plans we develop.

The future is something we both fancy and fear. All of our hopes dwell there, but that's also the direction we turn to with worries. More than one theologian has suggested that our experience of the future is the very shadow of God: the future holds our destiny. We can't turn away from it or control it. We just keep looking ahead, with hope and longing.

The attitudes one takes toward the future parallel stances taken toward God. For example, there's hope: I have quiet confidence that all will be well, because God, or the future, is provident. There's happenstance: I'm so afraid of the future that I race through the present. And then there's hell: I only want to be left alone. I want to close myself from all that is yet to come.

That's why I'm so amused with Rosalind Russell's way of delaying the inevitable future and full of compassion for the desire of Doubting Thomas to close himself off from it. After all, his teacher and friend was dead. Who hasn't handed a loved one into death's grasp and wanted to say, "Take me too! Without him (or her), what's left for me?"

Thomas is bitter, frightened, doubting. Of course he can't look ahead. His eyes are fixed on the past, rewinding and replaying what was always inevitable. We sometimes want to hunker down like Thomas. "Lord of the Future, leave me alone! I can't digest the past or stomach the present." But then *he* appears in a moment of grace. His wounds are still present; ours still smart. He smiles and one way or another says, "Put your finger here and see my hands. Reach out your hand and put it in my side. Do not doubt but believe" (John 20:27).

The old charmer! We don't want to answer that metaphorical divine phone. There must be a clever way to hide. But why hide? Because it is possible to see sufficiently that it is God and still to seek to avoid a positive response, even if this is done through self-prevarication. If knowledge of God compelled acceptance, the entire Christian understanding of faith would be scuttled. We're never compelled to choose God or God's ways, even if this means we choose something less than the human, less than what we ourselves truly can be. Sometimes it's just easier, or even much more pleasant, to hide. But then we hear God's voice. And someplace deep inside us unfolds, saying, "All right, one more round."

Let's close with Frye's Rosalind Russell. Here's a little vignette in which we see her embracing the future, answering that ringing phone if you will. She's found the strength to see what God asks of her and to respond with confidence in the life-giving goodness of God:

> [She] had two mastectomies, in 1960 and 1965. In 1969 she was hit with rheumatoid arthritis. In 1975 the cancer recurred.
>
> In August 1976, Gloria and Jimmy Stewart gave a party for Roz and 30 or 40 of her friends. Roz came in a gorgeous green spangled dress by Galanos, but she looked ill. Kirk Douglas and Jimmy Stewart and Jack Lemmon all made little speeches. Then Roz stood up. She looked around at us and said, "I have nothing here tonight but love. I love everybody in this room, and I know they love me. You know I haven't been well. But I'm here because dear Gloria and Jimmy planned this wonderful party. And you know what I'm thinking? I'm thinking that life is like a rope. It's tied with lots of knots, and it goes straight up. I have been climbing that rope, and each knot I come to is one of you. And then I climb to the next one. And to the next. I'm still holding on, and it's because of your love. So bless you all for coming and being with me here tonight."[7]

Henry Ball's Daughter

In February of 1915, Henry Durrell Ball, a telephone lineman, died of typhoid fever at the age of twenty-eight. He left behind a pregnant widow, Desirée, age twenty-two, and a toddling daughter. Trying to arrange her husband's affairs and the funeral, Desirée deposited her daughter in the care of a kindly grocer, a Mr. Flower. Six decades later the daughter would gratefully remember him: "He let me prance up and down his counter, reciting little pieces my parents had taught me. My favorite was apparently a frog routine where I hopped up and down harrumphing. Then I'd gleefully accept the pennies or candy Mr. Flower's customers would give me—my first professional appearance!"[8]

At the age of three-and-a-half, Henry Ball's daughter had learned to meet adversity with an entertaining smile. The world would come to know that smile and to love her. Her name was Lucille, Lucille Ball. Of course the world would simply learn to say, "I love Lucy."

We drain the power of the Gospel if we draw the line between the interior and the exterior of the human person in the wrong place. The great German theologian Karl Rahner insisted that we not think of ourselves as ending with our skin. The human person is more than just the thing we see before us. We were all given a sack of skin at birth, but what makes us unique, what truly forms our innards, is what we've done since then. Each of us is an unrepeatable, vast horizon of memories, talents, imagination, and desires.

In other words, our insides are formed by our interaction with the world. Spend hours at the piano, and you become a pianist. Athletes are honed by hours of exercise. We are what we read. We are who we know. We become what we do. All of that said, the Gospel challenge is to seek out those experiences that form the person God dreamt of and to eschew those that would deface that vision.

Lucille's maternal grandfather, Fred Hunt, used to tell her stories of New York City where dreams came true. Her biographer Stefan Kanfer writes that Lucille was not friendless in primary school, "still, the notion that she was poorer than her classmates kept her withdrawn and self-conscious. More than once she left the room for a drink of water and kept on going toward what she thought was Manhattan until someone spotted the child and brought her back."[9]

At that point, what the world would come to know of Lucille Ball was still inside her, struggling to emerge. But inside/outside isn't such a difficult equation to solve. What's inside is simply what we want of the outside, and that makes all the difference. It did for Lucy, and it does for us.

Like my friend Patti, Lucille Ball felt the call of God. It was aching to be released in her smile. Grace isn't something imported into our world. It's the foundation of that world. And "the call" isn't an ethereal ringing phone. It's the deep desire, the movements of the human heart. The Spirit plays the heart the way a master musician plays an instrument, the way Lucy "played" her comic face. Divine inspiration is not insertion into foreign ground. It is God-given insight and the energy and courage to respond to that insight.

Days of Our Lives

Let me begin by admitting that I am not proud of what I am about to tell you, and the fact that it began when I was a kid is no excuse. At first my sister and I were home alone and didn't know what we were getting into. Yet by high school I would hurry home at lunchtime from my summer job at the grocery store. If for some reason I missed, I could depend on my sister. Even now, I know that I can call and ask her: "What's up with Chloe and Phillip? Are they ever going to get together?"

Don't think I haven't tried to stop. I've gone years without watching *Days of Our Lives,* but then something happens. Before I know it, it's "Like sands through the hourglass, so are the days of our lives."[10] Once I went ten years without watching *Days.* I had only watched before then because the secretaries at the seminary watched it. What else were we supposed to talk about at lunch? But then one day in early fall the television was on. I looked up, and there was Hope Brady, finally happily married to Bo. Who could have predicted that? It had seemed a hopeless dream ten years earlier, when she had been kidnapped by the evil Stephano Dimeara. But wait, they weren't so happily married. Someone had switched J. T., their newborn baby, at birth, and, somewhere in the ten years that I had been gone, Hope had been someone named Princess Gina, someone who did terrible things, and if Stephano should reactivate the memory chip in her brain, she might yet go wayward again.

I know you're wondering, why would anyone let his emotions be wrung through this weekday wringer? But you don't understand what a comfort it was to see Grandma Horton, still reigning as the matriarch of the Horton clan. And Dr. Marlena Evans didn't look a day older! Sometimes at night I sit bolt upright in bed and ask, what do Deidra Hall and Susan Lucci know that I don't? How do they do it? One day they dragged out poor old Mickie Horton. I can remember when Mickie was young and handsome and married to Laura, before she went to the insane asylum. How long ago was that? Let's see. We were at war, and LBJ was president.

Maybe that's what draws me back. Every season there are new characters, new story lines that play themselves out over the space of a year or two, but there are also characters who have been with the show for decades. Here they are, still valiantly living the days of their lives, still hoping that this Christmas everyone in Salem will be happy and out of trouble. Sure, I want to scream at the set, "He's no good for you!—Can't you see she's lying?—Of course she stole your baby!" But I can't help hoping along with these folk.

Of course real life is not a soap opera. On a soap opera everyone has perfect hair, because stylists are always on duty. Every man who takes off his shirt has washboard abs, and women never wear the same dress twice. I don't know why real life isn't like that, but I think it's part of what we mean by original sin. Something is terribly wrong with our programming.

What is interesting about real life is the way we keep plodding on, week after month after year. Even plodders need a pause, and the church provides it, weekly and annually. *Gaudete* Sunday is that midpoint in December's Advent season when the church insists that we rejoice, and not because we're halfway through Advent, as though the strain of the thing were ever so much to bear. And we don't rejoice because Christ and Christmas are almost here. Advent is not about playacting at being Jewish, pretending that we have no messiah and then, come Christmas, surprise, we do! That might work as a child's explanation for the season, but its chief adult difficulty is simply the fact that it's not true.

The adult issue is this: we claim that the Messiah came some two thousand years ago. The challenge to that assertion is very simple. Where is that kingdom of God the Messiah should have brought? Where's the peace, the love, the contentment? Yes, of course, it begins in our hearts—nice sentiment—but how does that make Christianity any different from any other religion or self-help movement? Why rejoice that peace begins in the heart when it clearly hasn't begun in enough hearts? What is the difference between saying that no messiah has come and asserting that one came two thousand years ago but hasn't yet cleaned out Dodge City like any self-respecting messiah would? Why does the church tell us to rejoice?

Go back to what a soap opera shares with real life. On a soap opera, the good people suffer many setbacks. Sometimes a noble and beloved character dies, but the good only grows stronger through the drama of fighting evil. Who'd watch if the good didn't triumph in the ever-elusive end?

When we wait for the feast of Christmas and the kingdom of love Christ promised, the church insists that one is coming as surely as the other. What's the source of the joyful confidence? Before naming it, make sure you don't underestimate it. Despite the divorce rate, it will propel countless Christian couples to profess wedding vows in the coming year, and the wedding of two believers is propelled by more than human love. For better or worse, lovers no longer need vows simply to live together, which to my mind makes vows today all the more extraordinary, because vows speak of hope and confidence in the future.

That same confidence will carry newborn babes to innumerable baptismal fonts. Neither the church nor the world may be perfect, but those parents believe that both the world and the church belong to Christ, and they want the same to be said of their children, that they are Christ's own. Christian confidence will also be present when young men place their hands between the palms of a bishop and promise to live lives of poverty, chastity, and obedience. And, unless this year is utterly different from every single year of the

church's long history, the same confidence will pour forth from
Christian martyrs as freely as their blood.

What's the source? What reason is there for confidence and
hope? Because we believe the Messiah has come, not to end the
drama but to reign over it by reigning through it. In a sense, a Christian does think life to be a bit like a soap. The script was written
some two thousand years ago, fixed as firmly as Christ's hands were
to the cross. The happy ending became a certainty with the first
light of Easter. Soap operas offer a simple but winning formula:
lots of drama with an assured happy ending. And, did you ever
notice, that's also the message of the Gospel?

Why Aren't the Saints in the Soaps?

There's a good question. The saints would be naturals for daytime
TV! A sixteenth-century cannonball hits a man in the leg, and suddenly he finds religion: St. Ignatius of Loyola. A young soldier has an
argument with his father over money, disowns his dad, and takes off
all his clothes in the thirteenth-century town square: St. Francis of
Assisi. They remind the young woman one more time: "Remember,
you are not to speak to the Holy Father. Just kiss his ring and wait for
the blessing." She melodramatically throws herself at the nineteenth-
century pope's feet and begs permission to enter the convent of Carmel at age fifteen: St. Thérèse of Lisieux. A young man fathers an
illegitimate child and has the audacity to give him the lovely fourth-
century name, *Adeodatus,* meaning "God given": St. Augustine.

Why aren't the saints in the soaps? These were passionate men
and women. I think of St. Clare of Assisi writing to St. Agnes of
Prague, telling her that she is the spouse, the mother, and the sister
of Jesus Christ. I think of St. Mechthild of Magdeburg—okay fine,
she needs an agent, even among Catholics—writing, "Lord, you
are my lover, my longing, my flowing stream, my sun, and I am your
reflection."[11] I think of St. John of the Cross on his deathbed, the
penitential psalms being recited by the grieving friars; he raises his
head to ask that they recite instead that great Old Testament love

song, the Song of Songs, telling them that at last he is entering the bridal chamber, the one he has spent his life awaiting.

What makes a saint *into a saint* and the rest of us into, well, the rest of us? Passion! Desire! Longing! Often it's a broken heart, one determined never to settle again for less than everything. St. Elizabeth Ann Seton buried her husband in a nineteenth-century cemetery and then gave her heart to a lover death could never conquer. St. Augustine penned what may well be the most beautiful love lines ever written:

> Late have I loved you, O Beauty ever ancient, ever new, late have I loved you! You were within me, but I was outside, and it was there that I searched for you. In my unloveliness I plunged into the lovely things which you created. You were with me, but I was not with you. Created things kept me from you; yet if they had not been in you they would not have been at all. You called, you shouted, and you broke through my deafness. You flashed, you shone, and you dispelled my blindness. You breathed your fragrance on me; I drew in breath and now I pant for you. I have tasted you, now I hunger and thirst for more. You touched me, and I burned for your peace.[12]

Why are the saints so full of passion, so ardent with desire? Because they discovered a simple truth. Desire for God, intense hunger for God, finally brings us to God. God is fire. God does not warm the tepid. God is passion. God knows nothing of half-hearted love. In a vision God said to St. Mechthild: "It is my nature that makes me love you often, for I am love itself. It is my longing that makes me love you intensely, for I yearn to be loved from the heart. It is my eternity that makes me love you long. For I have no end."[13]

The saints should be in the soaps. Where else could one find so much relentless passion? Maybe they got it from the prophets:

> Therefore, I will now allure her,
>   and bring her into the wilderness,
>   and speak tenderly to her.
> From there I will give her her vineyards,
>   and make the Valley of Achor a door of hope.

There she shall respond as in the days of her youth,
> as at the time when she came out of the land of Egypt.
> (Hos 2:14-15)

Where did the saints ever get the idea that God should be like that? So ardent, so intense? Perhaps from that passionate virgin of Nazareth, the one who called himself the bridegroom. Because the irony is that even the passion of the saints for God pales in comparison with the desire for our love revealed in the person of Jesus. Jesus is the profligate lover, the one who throws away caution and calculation in the name of love.

2

Grace

What You Need to Know You Can Learn from Watching Audrey Hepburn Movies

Audrey Hepburn on Grace

The good news about Christian spirituality is that everything you really need to know about grace you can learn from watching Audrey Hepburn movies. Why? Because grace, even the *amazing* kind, always involves a type of knowing. It's a moment of insight and clarity into our relationship with God. After all, God doesn't change when we're graced. We do. God is always giving; God is always gift. Grace involves our opening up, not God's. Perhaps it helps to contrast the knowing that is grace from two other types of human knowledge.

First, there's the knowledge of discovery. You didn't know something, because it wasn't a part of your world. You had to go out and find it. Think of Audrey in *Roman Holiday* as Princess Ann. There she is, visiting the Eternal City on a goodwill tour, but she's a bit weary of being a princess who has no idea how ordinary folk live. So she takes up with Gregory Peck, playing the newspaper reporter Joe Bradley.

Princess Ann: "I could do some of the things I've always wanted to."

Joe Bradley: "Like what?"

"Oh, you can't imagine. I—I'd do just whatever I liked all day long."

"Tell you what. Why don't we do all those things, together?"

"But don't you have to work?"

"Work? No. Today's gonna be a holiday."

"But you want to do a lot of silly things?"

Joe takes the hand of the Princess. "First wish? One sidewalk café, comin' right up. I know just the place. Rocca's."[1]

And off they go to discover why God gave poor people gelato.

Or think of Eliza Doolittle in *My Fair Lady.* She doesn't know how to be a lady and has to learn. Those aristocratic vowels must be conquered. Professor Henry Higgins tells her:

> Eliza, you are to stay here for the next six months learning to speak beautifully, like a lady in a florist's shop. At the end of six months you will be taken to an embassy ball in a carriage, beautifully dressed. If the king finds out you are not a lady, you will be taken to the Tower of London, where your head will be cut off as a warning to other presumptuous flower girls! If you are not found out, you shall be given a present of . . . uh . . . seven and six to start life with in a lady's shop. If you refuse this offer, you will be the most ungrateful, wicked girl, and the angels will weep for you."[2]

It's a daunting task, becoming a proper lady, but it's still essentially simply a matter of discovering something you don't yet know.

In the same way, the young Prince Solomon, of Old Testament fame, knows that he doesn't really know how to be a king, even though that's the role he's just landed; he has to learn, so he prays that God grant him wisdom. "O Lord my God, you have made your servant king in place of my father David, although I am only a little child; I do not know how to go out or come in. And your servant is in the midst of the people whom you have chosen, a great people, so numerous they cannot be numbered or counted. Give your servant therefore an understanding mind to govern your people, able to discern between good and evil; for who can govern this your great people?" (1 Kgs 3:7-9). That knowledge is also called discovery. We all learn to do it, just like Audrey and the future King Solomon.

But then there's the knowledge we call *insight*. It's not about discovering something unknown in the world, not about adding a new piece of knowledge. Instead the pieces you already have co-alesce into a pattern that finally makes sense. You see something and, as you do, you realize that it was always there. St. Paul wants the Romans to come to insight when he tells them: "We know that all things work together for good for those who love God, who are called according to his purpose" (Rom 8:28). The idea here is that, if they would only let the pattern form, they'd see what's already there, what's always been there, namely grace, just like Audrey experiences in *Sabrina*.

Even as the child he never noticed, Sabrina has been infatuated with David Larrabee (William Holden), a spoiled and self-centered playboy. It takes the whole movie before she realizes that the person she should love, the person she does love, is his older, hardworking brother Linus (Humphrey Bogart). Nothing (no-thing) changes in Sabrina's world, only her insight into that world.[3]

Grace happens when you discover your place in the world, and something as big as that only occurs when someone as big as God steps in. Finding your place in the world isn't the same thing as moving from Texas to New York the way Audrey does as Holly Golightly in *Breakfast at Tiffany's*. It's finding your spot in a nest of relationships. It's the feeling of belonging that love brings.

Most of the time we're just like Holly at the beginning of the movie. We don't suffer from the blues so much as what she calls "the mean reds." We're afraid of something we can't even name. She says, "The blues are because you're getting fat and maybe it's been raining too long, you're just sad that's all. The mean reds are horrible. Suddenly you're afraid and you don't know what you're afraid of."[4] That's what it feels like to be lost in the world. You haven't heard the call or recognized the face. You haven't found the love that sets the disparate features of your life in order, like beautifully arranged diamonds in a tennis bracelet from Tiffany's.

Here's how Holly explains her feline's name to Paul Varjak, played by George Peppard: "He's all right! Aren't you, cat? Poor cat! Poor slob! Poor slob without a name! The way I see it I haven't got the right to give him one. We don't belong to each other. We just took up one day by the river. I don't want to own anything until I find a place where me and things go together. I'm not sure where that is but I know what it is like. It's like Tiffany's."

But, at the end of the movie, Holly realizes that the only way to find a place in the world is to love and be loved by others. That's why she doesn't fly off to Brazil but instead comes back to love Paul Varjak and Cat, who is all wet because she threw him out of the cab.

In *My Fair Lady* Henry Higgins has his own moment of grace, finds his spot in the world, when he has to admit, "I've grown accustomed to her face." For him the realization has dawned that Eliza's face is the world. It's *his* world. Grace happens when you look at the world that you share with everyone else and suddenly find a spot—really a whole world in that little spot—that is uniquely your own. And sometimes that world can be wonderfully summed up in a single face.

Grace is a form of knowing, but it's different from discovery or mere insight. You don't find something new in the world, and you don't just see the world in a new way. You find your place in the world. Love steps in and claims you, and love has a way of reordering sight. That's why we say that lovers see the world through rose-colored glasses or that the birth of a child changes everything.

After giving a number of complex analogies to describe the kingdom of God, Jesus asks, "Have you understood all this?" (Matt 13:51). Jesus asks this question *in* Matthew's gospel (the individual book) and, one could say, asks this question *of* the Gospel (God's message writ large). The Gospel is about the proclamation that love has sought us out, that love has found us. A person who has encountered the grace of the Gospel, one who knows that the Gospel is the very offer of grace, is finally free to live in the world in a radically different way. We sell it all to buy the field with the treasure, or to obtain the priceless pearl, and those beyond the glow of grace can't get a glimmer of what we're up to.

At the end of *The Nun's Story*, Audrey leaves behind her life as Sister Luke and returns to the world as Gabrielle van der Mal. Good Catholics are of course disappointed, but sometimes even good Catholics have trouble recognizing that we don't, we simply can't, labor to win God's love. It comes as a gift. Sister Luke tells Mother Christophe (Beatrice Straight), "I thought that one would reach some sort of resting place where obedience would be natural and struggle would end."

And Mother Christophe wisely answers, "There is no final resting place, ever. But you must have patience with yourself."[5] It's not a question of getting to a spot where we can claim God's love. It's about finding the spot, the right relationships, where we can finally see God's love. Learn that, and you've been graced. You've heard the Gospel. And you can thank Audrey Hepburn!

Reading the Whole Script

Do you recognize the name William Frawley? If not, you probably would if I added the names of his co-stars: Vivian Vance, Desi Arnaz, and Lucille Ball. Did you know that William Frawley was only reluctantly hired to play the role of Fred Mertz, the irascible landlord and friend of Ricky and Lucy Ricardo? He was hired reluctantly because he had a reputation for excessive drinking. Desi Arnaz took a chance on him but let it be known that a drunk actor would soon be an unemployed one. According to Stefan Kanfer, Desi told him: "The first time you are not able to do your job, I'll try to work around you for that day. The second time, I'll try to manage again. But if you do it three times, then you are through, and I mean *through*, not only on our show, but you'll never work in this town again as long as you live. Is that fair enough?"[6]

In *Ball of Fire,* his biography of Lucille Ball, Stefan Kanfer writes:

> What viewers saw on the screen was not very different from what the performers dealt with on the set. Upon presentation of the script, Frawley would take home only the pages marked FRED, in order to memorize his lines. "So sometimes," Desi recollected, "we would get to a joke and he would say to me, 'This is not funny.'
>
> 'What do you mean?' I'd ask. 'It's not funny? You haven't read the five other pages where we have been building up to your entrance.'
>
> 'What are you talking about?'
>
> 'You're just reading what you are supposed to say and we've been building up for you to come in and say, "Hello, Ethel," and get a big laugh.'
>
> 'You think "Hello, Ethel" is funny?'
>
> 'No, "Hello, Ethel" is not funny, but we've been building up this situation in which Ethel is inside a costume, representing the last half of a horse, and as you come in the door, she is bending down and facing away from you. All you can see is the last half of this horse—the horse's ass is all you can see—and you say, "Hello Ethel," and *that* is funny.'
>
> 'Oh, yes, that *is* funny!'"[7]

The prophet Isaiah promised that our God would come to open the eyes of the blind and that the ears of the deaf would be cleared (35:4-5). Open eyes and ready ears have a lot to do with a word you've probably used since childhood but might be hard-pressed to define, one I've used repeatedly. It's a simple word, "grace." Desi's treatment of William Frawley was an act of grace. When we do find our place in the world—even if it takes time to recognize that we have indeed found that place—we realize that we've received more than we deserve or could hope for. We've experienced love from another, and then we recognize a second face behind the face we love, a divine face full of love.

The catechism says that "grace is *favor,* the *free and undeserved help* that God gives us to respond to his call to become children of

God."[8] That seems quite straightforward until one asks just what sort of a thing grace is. We tend to picture grace, like some moonbeam or energy ray, flowing into our bodies, though we do realize that there's something wrong with that picture.

The Hebrew roots of our word grace, *hanan* and *hesed,* both suggest a favoring on the part of God. We recognize that God has acted on our behalf. That being said, it's helpful to jettison the picture of grace as an object and try to think of grace as an event. It's that moment when we recognize the presence of God in our lives, when finally, and all too briefly, we realize that God has always been there working on our behalf.

One could say that grace is a moment akin to seeing the entire script of the play, rather than just one small portion. We see what might be called "the whole" rather than just a part, and we perceive the very presence of God. When that's understood, it's easy to see why Christians insist that Jesus himself is the foremost of God's graces. When one's eyes are opened to see who he is, one understands him to be the very revelation of God's favor, God's action on our behalf.

William Frawley never lost his job on *I Love Lucy* because of drinking. Somehow he realized that he had been given the chance of a lifetime to play Fred Mertz. He couldn't lose that opportunity. It was his pearl of great price, and he seized it. Realization, insight, is the beginning of salvation. One could say it is grace itself. Because with grace the insight that dawns is not of human origin. It's the intuition that what we most desperately need in order to survive and thrive in life has already been given.

The Return of the King

Have you ever looked at your room through a mirror? Or, before digital cameras, peered into the negative of a photo? Or simply examined any photo and realized that you don't part your hair on the side that your mirror says you do? Those could be called small sensations of possessing the same old world in a different way. The

German existentialist philosopher Martin Heidegger used to speak of our "fallenness," always insisting that he was writing not of sin but of something equally lethal, the inability to see the world as it is, because our relationship with the world has grown coarse, common. We become so accustomed to the world that we fail to encounter the world. His famous example: who thinks about the hammer until it breaks? Like any other folk, Christians can suffer from the same sort of "everyday blindness." We can fail to see the world, the communion that is the church, Holy Communion itself, for the gifts that they are.

The experience of grace is always one of insight. Remember Audrey Hepburn's Sabrina? When she finally sees Linus Larrabee (played by Humphrey Bogart) for whom he really is, it's not her world that changes but her perception of it, her ability to engage it. With grace we suddenly see what we did not see before. I say "suddenly see" because grace always presents itself as something unearned, unexpected, coming from outside ourselves. We perceive something previously occluded. It was there, but we missed the configuration. And then understanding grasps what, before, hadn't even been noticed. The church has always taught that grace pervades the world. To quote the Jesuit poet Gerald Manley Hopkins, "The world is charged with the grandeur of God. / It will flame out, like shining from shook foil."[9]

J. R. R. Tolkien wrote, "It was in fairy-stories [his word for what today would be called fantasy or science fiction] that I first divined the potency of words, and the wonder of all things, such as stone, and wood, and iron; trees and grass, house and fire, bread and wine."[10] Tolkien always insisted that fantasy stories do not belong primarily to children. On the contrary, their purpose is to help adults see their own world, sometimes for the first time, simply by recasting it.

Tolkien's view of the world was behind the trilogy that even caustic critics couldn't help but call the cinematic epic of our times, *The Lord of the Rings*. People have their diverse reasons for seeing the three movies: the landscapes, the special effects, the masterfully choreographed battle scenes. But Tolkien suggested another reason for the popularity of his saga. He wrote that in fantasy one gets a "fleeting glimpse of Joy, Joy beyond the walls of the world."[11]

Unlike C. S. Lewis' *The Chronicles of Narnia*, Tolkien spurned allegory. One isn't supposed to read his tale and say, "this represents that." The story stands on its own, yet it's infused with Tolkien's own conservative Catholicism. He wrote, "I have consciously planned very little; and should be chiefly grateful for having been brought up (since I was eight) in a Faith that has nourished me and taught me all the little that I know." That faith, he insisted, "I owe to my mother, who clung to her conversion and died young, largely through the hardships of poverty resulting from it."[12] When Tolkien's mother converted to Catholicism, her wealthy family cut off all financial support to the widow and her two boys.

It was C. S. Lewis who wrote, "The heart of Christianity is a myth which is also a fact."[13] By myth he meant an epic of such grandeur that it inspires. Tolkien knew the Christian myth to be a fact, and therefore he created a new myth that, by allowing us to see the grandeur of Christianity, would then confront us with the sheer fact of Christianity. "The Christian joy, the Gloria," he said, "is pre-eminently (infinitely, if our capacity were not finite) high and joyous."[14]

We know that good and evil swirl in the world around us. More than that, we know that they struggle for possession of the world within us. The graced magic at work in *The Lord of the Rings* is that we think we are viewing a different, fantastic world, when we have really only encountered ourselves in a unique mirror of the soul.

Good and evil struggle for dominion of Middle Earth, but they also wage war within the soul of Frodo the Hobbit. He receives a ring of power that would allow him to become invisible and dominate the world. He must struggle to destroy the ring before it destroys him, as it did his predecessor, Sméagol, who, once fallen, becomes the Gollum. Who can't see the parallels? A ring of power that allows one to step out of the world in order to dominate it, a tree of the knowledge of good and evil, a poor soul who wants to control the world and finds himself dominated by power itself. How is the gollum different from Adam? A little hobbit who holds the fate of his world in his hand? A powerless Palestinian whose hands are nailed to the wood of the cross. A once and future king. A wizard who speaks words of prophecy while passing from death to life. A lady whose intercession is never sought in vain? One would have to be bewitched by Sauron himself not to see the parallels.

"Truly I tell you, no prophet is accepted in the prophet's hometown" (Luke 4:24). Had Heidegger been around, he could have explained the rejection of Jesus. Something within the world dulls our very possession of the world. We miss the offer of grace, which is the revelation that the world comes from love, that love beckons us to receive itself in the world. We can miss that offer as surely as those Nazarenes spurned the author of grace. One might say that *The Lord of the Rings* is one more way of fulfilling the injunction God gave Jeremiah: "But you, gird up your loins; stand up and tell them everything that I command you" (1:17). The word will find a way.

Many producers before Peter Jackson wanted the rights to Tolkien's trilogy, but he was always appalled by what he considered to be their leveling intent. One translated *lembas,* the bread that the Elves give to Sam and Frodo to sustain their journey to Mount Doom, as "food concentrate." Tolkien responded that *lembas* was beyond chemical analysis. It "has a larger significance, of what might hesitatingly be called a 'religious kind.'"[15] Properly translated *lembas* means "way-bread" or "life-bread."

The next time you go to the altar of God, try to see what you perhaps haven't seen before, and ponder this passage from *The Return of the King:*

> The *lembas* has a virtue without which they would long ago have lain down to die. It did not satisfy desire, and at times Sam's mind was filled with memories of food, and the longing for simple bread and meats. And yet this waybread of the Elves had a potency that increased as travelers relied on it alone and did not mingle it with other foods. It fed the will, and it gave strength to endure, and to master sinew and limb beyond the measure of mortal kind.[16]

Isn't that the gift we receive in the Eucharist? Isn't Tolkien simply removing the commonplace so that we can see a Christic cosmos, one suffused with gifts, one full of blessings? Isn't Eucharist, the church's great act of thanksgiving, a way of seeing and saying this world is a gift?

Diana Leaves the World

I took two books with me on my last vacation, Pope Benedict's *Jesus of Nazareth* and Tina Brown's *The Diana Chronicles.* I can report that both are excellent reads, trying, as they do, to discover the person behind the legend, though I must confess that the pages turned a little faster reading the life of Princess Diana. Sorry, Lord! I guess I figured you had fewer secrets.

Maybe we buy the biographies of celebrities because they allow us to try on other lives. Perhaps surprisingly, Tina Brown manages to convince most readers that they would not want to change places with the former Princess of Wales, because becoming princess essentially meant turning her back on the world. Consider, for example, this passage, describing Diana's honeymoon aboard the Royal Yacht *Britannia*:

> When he wrote from *Britannia* to friends, [the prince] . . . talked of his young wife like a grandfather about his teenage granddaughter: "Diana dashes about chatting up all the sailors and cooks in the gallery etc. while I remain hermit-like on the verandah deck, sunk with pure joy into one of Laurens van der Post's books."
>
> Diana below stairs dashing *abite,* of course, meant she was bored out of her mind with the company of A deck. And who can blame her? She loved the swimming and the sun, but the only other thing to do on the boat was read, and books had never been her long suit. At night the couple were liable to be joined for dinner by a phalanx of crisp, rippling *Britannia* senior officers on their best behavior and serenaded by a mood-enhancing medley of the Royal Marines. There was no pulling into port to hit the cafés and shops as they cruised past the seaside playgrounds of the Mediterranean. Aside

from the complications of the press, *Britannia* showing up means the Crown Is in Town. The royal yacht could not visit foreign soil without being met and feted by local dignitaries. In Port Said, they had to welcome the President of Egypt, Anwar Sadat, and his wife, Jihan, aboard for dinner.[17]

I suspect that most young girls, like Diana, dream of being a princess someday, but I doubt that many picture their honeymoons including dinner with Anwar Sadat. Yet the more one reads of Diana's ascent to privilege, the more her journey seemed to demand a turning away from the world, eschewing the simple pleasures that you and I take for granted.

There are Christians who see the path of discipleship in much the same way, as a renunciation of the world and all its pleasures. And there's plenty of Scripture to support that view. Service to the Lord meant imprisonment for the prophet Jeremiah, exile for Isaiah. It brought death to John the Baptist. Did it leave any biblical servant unscathed? And Jesus himself, in the Gospel of Luke, seems virtually to declare war on the world when he asserts, "I came to bring fire to the earth, and how I wish it were already kindled!" (12:49).

Christians who think the modern world is on its way to hell can find plenty of verses to quote. Indeed, in John's gospel, the very word "world" is used to designate whatever stands opposed to the person of Jesus, and much and many do.

And yet—and it's a gloriously big yet—it's John's gospel that boldly proclaims the so-often-quoted statement: "For God so loved the world that he gave his only Son, so that everyone who believes in him may not perish but may have eternal life" (3:16). And there's the deepest truth of the Gospel. The world is only condemned inasmuch as its stands in opposition to the gift of Christ, but the world itself is deeply loved. It's veritably worthy of love, because it comes forth as a gift from God. To be Christian does not mean to disdain the world. Christ didn't. He took on its flesh; he entered its history; he died for its denizens.

To be Christian doesn't demand hating contemporary fashion, culture, or pleasures. Remember, the strongest criticism his enemies threw at him was that Jesus was a glutton and a drunk (Matt 11:19; Luke 7:34).

We're asked only to turn from that which deals death, because being Christian demands living life to the fullest. No doubt there are some Christians who would disagree with my drift, seeing it as abandoning their agenda of hating the modern world, but that's simply not the essence of Christianity. Pope Benedict says we can find that essence in the Beatitudes. (See, I did read the other book.) Listen to him discussing the attitude of a Christian toward God, an attitude he feels the Beatitudes describe so perfectly. It's not about hating the world. It's about thanking God for the gift of this world, one created by God and redeemed in the cross of Christ. You can't see the world as a gift and spend your energy hating the world as something less than God. If you can sing along with Louis Armstrong's "What a Wonderful World"—the song I want belted out at my funeral—you can't set up an opposition between God and God's greatest gift. The Gospel of John appears to set up this opposition by using the word "world" as a type of shorthand for that which rejects God's initiative in Jesus. But that doesn't mean one can't find the world itself to be suffused with the love of God. After all, Jesus himself did just that! The pope talks about emptying hands (of things like pretension, arrogance, obduracy) so that we can receive from God's own goodness. He writes of humble Christians:

> These are people who do not flaunt their achievements before God. They do not stride into God's presence as if they were partners able to engage with him on an equal footing; they do not lay claim to a reward for what they have done. They are people who know that their poverty also has an interior dimension; they are lovers who simply want to let God bestow his gifts upon them and thereby to live in inner harmony with God's nature and word. The saying of Saint Thérèse of Lisieux about one day standing before God with empty hands, and holding them open to him, describes the spirit of these poor ones of God. They come with empty hands, not with

hands that grasp and clutch, but with hands that open and give and thus are ready to receive from God's bountiful goodness.[18]

It's not a question of hating the world. It's a question of receiving this world, and the next, as God's good gift.

It's sad to think that Diana was asked to surrender the world for a crown. Yet we remember her because she refused the sacrifice. She continued to love the little pleasures that you and I take for granted. And I don't think one could describe our cat-loving, piano-playing, and so-stylishly-dressing current pope as someone who hates life's blessings.

No, it's not about hating the world. It's all about falling in love with the giver of such a gift. And then, of course, there's no telling what we might sacrifice—but in the name of love, not disdain.

Archie Leach

As he tells it, "My father made no more than a modest living and we had little money." He remembers

> being awakened late one evening by the noise of a party far below in the drawing room, and of my father's coming up and carrying me downstairs on his shoulders to be shown off to the guests and to lisp unhappily and haltingly through the first poem I ever learned. There I was wrapped in a blanket reciting *Up in a Balloon So High* while my father, showing both pride and strength at the same time, held me at arm's length high above his head in the air. It was a high-ceilinged room and I remember being very close to the high center chandelier. I think my father was high too.[19]

Archie Leach's father was a tall man with a fancy moustache; his mother, "a dark haired beauty." Biographers seem to speak of more tension between the parents than Archie does in his autobiography. What was the trouble? It seems that his father chafed at both his limited circumstances and his withdrawn wife. When Archie was nine, his father took a job away from Bristol and most probably took up with another woman.

His father did eventually return, but his parents' relationship did not improve. One day the nine-year-old boy came home to be told by cousins that his mother had gone away to a seaside resort. As the weeks went by and she did not return, his father finally confided to him that she had died, presumably of a heart attack.

Raised more by relatives than his father, who was now free to pursue his own life, at the age of fourteen Archie Leach forged his father's signature and joined an acrobatic troop, which eventually brought him to America and the Great White Way. But it was Hollywood that would give the young man his new name and the fame that came with it.

More than twenty years later, a renamed Archie Leach returned to Bristol as Cary Grant and reconnected with an aging, alcoholic father. Sometimes you can only move forward by retracing your steps. You have to go back and face what you fled. But there was another connection he did not expect to make. His father told him that his mother was alive. She had not died of a heart attack years before. Perhaps in pursuit of his freedom, perhaps not, his father had had her committed for health reasons that today seem dubious. It's hard to imagine a father exercising such control over a young man's life. To find his own peace and place, Elias James Leach had excised his wife from his own life and that of his son.

Jesus says, "Are not two sparrows sold for a small coin? Yet not one of them will fall to the ground apart from your Father['s knowledge]" (Matt 10:29). He seems almost to present us with a father more draconian in control than that of Cary Grant. And Christian theology will follow Jesus in attributing all things to God. Under the influence of Sacred Scripture, St. Thomas Aquinas will part ways with Aristotle and insist that God is the *efficient* cause of the world, meaning that nothing would exist without the Fatherhood of God. Aristotle had called God the *formal* cause of a world that he considered to be eternal. For him, God didn't bring the world into existence, but God, being that which is most perfect and most worthy of love, draws all things within the world to God's self. Of course Aristotle's God was too perfect even to have intercourse with the world. He dwelt in eternal, unmovable bliss. He couldn't hear the prayers of earth.

Aristotle's God is clearly not the Father of Jesus, and so St. Thomas acknowledged a second gift of God, one equally as marvelous as creation itself. Of all the creatures on earth, we alone have been endowed with freedom. God who creates the world also creates space within the world for what might be called the drama of human history, the dialogue of divine and human love. Aquinas will thus speak of a God who is the efficient cause of the world's existence and the formal cause of its dynamism. He withdraws enough to create freedom, but he sends the Son as an answer to prayer, as one who teaches us that God does answer prayer. One could say that we have been given a world that is free, but not godless.

Perhaps the hardest thing a father, or any parent, does is to acknowledge when the moment has come to withdraw. A good father must do things, like take his child to school, allow his boy to play his own sports, walk his daughter down the aisle into the arms of another. A good father gives two precarious, precious gifts: life and freedom. Without such fathers we would neither be nor be ourselves.

The French philosopher Jean-Luc Marion has suggested that distance is an essential quality in any relationship. He writes, "Only distance, in maintaining a distinct separation of . . . persons, renders communion possible, and immediately mediates the relation."[20] I take him to mean that any healthy relationship is characterized by a certain distance, a gap between one and the other that allows each to be his or her own self. Draw in the other too tightly, and you risk losing either yourself or the other. Marion insists, "One must admit a distance in order that the other may deploy in it the conditions of my union with him."[21] The other person needs room in the relationship to be him or herself, to be someone who isn't simply a projection of yourself and your needs. Without some distance, it's hard even to know what sort of relationship one has with another.

The next time you don't find God the first place you look, or can't understand why your plan of action doesn't seem to be God's, realize that love itself requires distance and deference. Would we really want a father as draconian as Grant's? One who simply decides our fate?

One more memory from Cary Grant, this one of his father doing a better job at fathering, giving life and letting go.

> One year I got a magic lantern with colored comic slides. I gave my only children's party because of acquiring that magic lantern. The only children's party I remember ever attending: my own. Father rigged up a sheet at the end of a back room which was usually used as a storage room, where the din would be less likely to disturb the district. Mother had some throw carpets, chairs, cushions and the long cloth-covered trestle table put in, and I invited our local infant world to my magic-lantern show. The lantern was candle-powered, a large candle with a large reflector behind it. Lemonade and biscuits and those inevitable tangerines, nuts, muscatels and dates were served, and blancmange and cake for dessert, because this was before the days of such luxuries as ice cream. We also had paper hats and noise-makers. It was a fine party.
>
> My father ran the show to avoid my setting fire to the house, I suppose; but I chose the order in which the slides were to be seen, and accompanied the showing of each with what I thought was appropriate comic comment. But I was so regularly drowned out by other comic commentators that I couldn't tell if I was a success or not. Perhaps that's why I eventually entered the movies: so that the audience couldn't talk back to me.[22]

A Question of Inspiration

Winter, 1942. German-occupied Holland. As atrocities mount, so does resistance to the German occupation. Even young children are drawn into acts of defiance. A young Dutch girl, not yet sixteen, a dance student who speaks English because of her absent British father, is asked to take a message to an English paratrooper hiding in the Arnhem forest. He cannot continue to hide there, because the Germans are about to swarm the woods in maneuvering exercises. She is to find the paratrooper and give him instructions on where to rendezvous with members of the resistance who will provide a new hiding place.

> She volunteered at once and entered the forest, calmly and innocently picking wildflowers as she went—a ruse in case she was stopped suddenly by a German soldier. . . . [She] found the paratrooper just where she was told, gave him the information, answered his questions and headed back for the village. As she did so, she was met by two of the enemy, who addressed her in German, pointing to the path from which she had emerged and asking for the reason for her presence in the area. Acting as if she had no idea what they wanted, she smiled brightly and handed them the bunch of flowers.

To her astonishment, "the soldier accepted the bouquet, patted her on her shoulder and sent her on her way."[23]

Though no one applauded and no cameras rolled, that was the first acting assignment for Audrey Hepburn. No director, no rehearsal, no script. Simply a sudden exigency and the birth of an astonishing ability to meet it. One more datum in the ongoing debate: Is greatness an innate gift or a honed craft? In this case, it would appear that whatever her future directors and acting partners would offer, they didn't create the actor of *Breakfast at Tiffany's* and *The Nun's Story*. They simply nurtured a gift of God. Grace came to a young Audrey Hepburn as recognition of what God wanted, what the situation required of her, and as the steady confidence that God would aid her.

Quick change of scene. Let's shift to that very person of the Trinity whom we think of as the very personification of grace, the Holy Spirit, and Pentecost, the Spirit's bestowal upon the church. Both are mysteries in search of an image. We can picture a baby lying in a manger. We know well enough how to comprehend the suffering of Good Friday. But Easter and Pentecost don't move us emotionally for the simple reason that we can't adequately picture those events. Imagining an empty tomb is easy enough, but how does one picture resurrection? Likewise, Pentecostal "tongues as of fire" is obviously a metaphor, but for something clearly beyond our ken. What happened in that upper room doesn't register in our imaginations, and, because we can't produce a picture that resonates with our own experience, we're left somewhat estranged from the very mystery that we celebrate.

It helps to remember that Pentecost is essentially an Easter mystery. The very name, derived from the Greek for "fifty days" is meant to link this mystery back to that of the empty tomb. The church asks us to ponder the meaning of resurrection for fifty days. Remembering that Pentecost closes the Easter season helps to locate the meaning of the feast. It's not an event that stands alone. Its significance can't be accessed apart from the events of Easter. One could say that Pentecost is the answer to this question: What is the relationship between the Spirit of God and that empty tomb?

When scholars initially asked that question in the first flush of the Enlightenment, they were so imbued with the progress of science that they were more than willing to jettison any explanation that seemed to go beyond the ken of rationalism. Hence, they explained away the resurrection by saying that it was simply a primitive way of asserting that the spirit of Jesus lived on, as an inspiration to his followers. There are lots of problems with that rationalistic and shallow hypothesis.

The first is the radical transformation in the behavior of his followers. By their own admission—an assertion scholars trust— his disciples were dispirited. They had fled his cause, having seen it wrecked against the immovable force of Rome. The question needing to be asked is how they could go, in the space of a weekend, from crushing disillusionment about Jesus to the radical, life-threatening assertion that he was alive. The scholars of the Enlightenment seem to have the causal sequence backwards. It wasn't belief in his message that led to the assertion that he lived. It was the assertion that he was alive that reinvigorated belief in the message.

Yet, unbelieving as they were, those Enlightenment scholars had identified a factor in the resurrection accounts that many Christians ignore: the question of inspiration. If the resurrection were simply something that happened to Jesus, it would never have become a pivotal moment in history. It's not enough to say that during the course of that Easter weekend the disciples became convinced of a fact, because people don't die for abstract facts, not even extraordinary ones. When people live and die, it is for more than a fact. It is because they have a conviction. Where did the conviction that Jesus was alive come from? Not simply from what they saw, Jesus alive before them, but also from what they felt within them. The disciples became infused, animated, possessed by a spirit not their own. Something happened in that empty tomb, something neither they, nor we, will ever fully understand. But it would have been nothing more than an unexplainable mystery if something hadn't also happened inside the disciples. They *felt* a spirit which, if one reads the earlier accounts, they simply called the Spirit of Jesus acting within them. He was alive in them. That's perhaps how they would have put it at first. Today we'd say that the Holy Spirit, his Holy Spirit, had come to dwell in them.

We have no analogue for such an experience. We've heard accounts of people, faced with a crisis, suddenly summoning up energies and talents they never knew they possessed, like young Audrey Hepburn in the Arnhem forest, but this is that and something more: a personal presence, the recognition that these powers were not the disciples' own, and that they came accompanied by the loving gaze of another.

The New Testament authors would stretch the Easter mystery into a sequence of fifty days, but the radical outpouring of this Spirit was immediately and undeniably linked to the tomb. Whatever had happened *in there* was happening *in them*. Years of reflection would lead to later formulations: that Jesus had been raised in the power of the Spirit, and that, as Paul tells the Romans, "the Spirit of God dwells in you" (Rom 8:9). We understand Pentecost better when we realize that, without the outpouring of the Spirit, Easter would be simply a mystery and not a mounting, radical call to conversion of life.

One could say that inside the young Audrey Hepburn, an actor was waiting for her moment, and I think that would be essentially correct. She felt the call of God, the movement of grace. Not through special revelation but by responding to the depth of her own humanity. She allowed her person and her talents to grow in tandem. What would later emerge was already there. But, by their own accounts, the disciples insisted that Easter represented something altogether different. The Spirit was not in their dispirited, broken lives. Not that Friday or that Saturday. It took an empty tomb to infuse those lives with more than meaning. In addition to their Jesus, something, someone came out of that tomb. A personal presence entered the world. It's one we've felt ourselves, though we still struggle to imagine it.

3

Love

A Play in Several Acts

Somewhere in My Youth or Childhood

One day, at the conclusion of my freshman Perspectives in Christianity class, a young woman appeared at my desk. She was one of the silent ones who never speak in class. We had just finished a rather energetic discussion of baptism, original sin, and faith. "Father, can I ask you a question?"

Her query went something like this: "If I believe in God—or believe in something—but I don't believe in the Catholic Church—or, I don't know that I don't believe in it, I just don't know if I do believe in it—anyway, if I died today, would God accept my soul or would I be damned?"

Just one of the simple questions students ask in the ten minutes between classes. This is what I said: "But in your own, unique way, you are responding to the offer God has made to you, as best you can, just now. You *are* searching. How could you be held responsible for not responding to the wonderful offer of love that God makes to you in the church until you understand that offer and who is making it?"

"So . . . I wouldn't be damned?"

"What kind of God would damn you for not saying 'yes' to what you don't yet understand? Hopefully, by the grace of God, the moment will come. You'll see the church as the very presence of Christ, and then you'll respond. It will be like falling in love with someone you hadn't noticed before. The moment of clarity will come, and it will be wonderful."

Had I had more than a couple of minutes, I might have quoted some words of Rogers and Hammerstein. As Maria, Julie Andrews sings them in the gazebo to Christopher Plummer, playing Captain von Trapp, when she realizes for the first time that she was created to love this man. It's not as though the time in the convent had been wasted, any more than his first marriage hadn't been providently provided and blessed by God. But stand before the one you love, and all of life up to that moment appears to be something of a dress rehearsal! In the words of Richard Rogers:

> Perhaps I had a wicked childhood,
> Perhaps I had a miserable youth.
> But somewhere in my wicked, miserable past
> There must've been a moment of truth.
> For here you are, standing there, loving me,
> Whether or not you should.
> So, somewhere in my youth or childhood
> I must have done something good.
> Nothing comes from nothing,
> Nothing ever could.
> So somewhere in my youth or childhood
> I must have done something good.[1]

It's when we see love, and *know* that we see love, that we are compelled to choose love. Even the baroness (Doris Lloyd) reluctantly admits to the captain, "There's nothing more irresistible to a man than a woman who's in love with him."

Here's how Maria explains her feelings for Captain von Trapp to the mother abbess, played by the incomparable Peggy Wood: "There were times when we would look at each other, oh Mother I could hardly breathe."

Yep, that's when we realize that we were made for this moment, the moment we either fling ourselves into the arms of love or withdraw into something of a selfish, simpering solitude. It's at that moment that our entire life appears graced, even those shadow lands we've never wanted to claim, never understood how we could claim.

How many years had the noble heart of St. Luke's tax collector Zacchaeus waited? How many places had he sought out the meaning of his life? But when he heard the words, "Zacchaeus, hurry and come down; for I must stay at your house today," he understood *who* was speaking and what he offered (Luke 19:5). The gospels are all about recognizing love and then risking everything to attain it.

The book of Wisdom asks, "How would anything have endured if you had not willed it? Or how would anything not called forth by you have been preserved? You spare all things, for they are yours, O Lord, you who love the living" (11:25). That's as good a name for God as any ever penned: "Lover of souls."

Christ is God's great offer of love, and he makes that offer through the fellowship we call the church. After all, Bibles don't jump off bookshelves at Barnes and Noble, saying, "Thank heaven you came down this aisle. I'm God's offer of self." No, the Bible comes forth from the mystery we call the church, and it would have no meaning without being continually received by that very same community of faith. Whether we first heard the Gospel from a preacher's pulpit or in our mothers' laps, we heard the voice of the church, offering the gift of Christ. Can one be damned for missing the offer through no fault of one's own? Who could love such a peremptory God? Why would such a God even be worthy of our worship?

But here's another question: When, like Zacchaeus, you do realize who is here in the communion of the church and what is offered, who could fail to love such a God?

Love Is My Name and My Home

It was one of the great discoveries of my childhood, which is why the scene remains fixed in my mind. My parents were in love!

I say it was a discovery, because like many children I found my progenitors somewhat difficult to understand. They just didn't fit the TV models I had been given. My father would occasionally call my mother "Honey," but on coming home from work he didn't sound off like Ward Cleaver on *Leave It to Beaver,* "Honey, I'm home."[2] When my father arrived home from the grocery store, he had just seen my mom an hour earlier when she left work at the same store to come home and fix supper. So he was much more likely to speak to us, to answer our endless questions about the contents of the grocery bag—sour cream and three cucumbers—or to give permission for me to use the rake for a robot I was building.

No, nothing in their demeanor suggested that they were in love. For example, in the bedroom, mom and dad shared a bed, which seemed quite peculiar, because Ricky and Lucy Ricardo didn't and neither did Rob and Laura Petrie. I surmised that there were two reasons for this: our family's poverty and my parents' generosity towards their children. And except on nights when I was afraid of the dark, I was very grateful that mom and dad had spent what little money they had to give the twin beds to my brother Harold and me.

If anything, my parents' bedroom was a source of friction, because that's where they wrestled. Often, late at night, I would hear my mother say, "Irvin, not yet." Or she'd say, "Irvin, stay on your side of the bed." This seemed quite out of character, because my dad was not one to "hog his share," as we would say in Kansas. Sadly, it would lead to a rumble and row. No bad words would be exchanged, but dad would eventually provoke mom into wrestling with him. Yes, I could hear it from my bedroom. Terrible thrashing about and, although Mom whimpered a bit, she seemed to hold her own for the longest time.

I might have guessed that my parents were in love when I watched them dance, though everything about wedding dances struck me as so resolutely different from ordinary life. Everyone—aunts, uncles, and cousins—happy, eating and drinking and dancing, and none of them talking about things like work or painting the house. When my parents danced, my father's back would arch, and he would get the oddest look on his face. He would concentrate, as if he were a soldier on parade, his own personality subsumed into the role and the routine. My mother always called it his "Gene Autry look." All that was left of Dad was an enormous smile.

As you can see, there was nothing to suggest love between my parents. No one hugged in our family. No one embraced or kissed among our relatives—we were Russian, Volga River Germans transplanted to Kansas—I'm not sure it was legal. Uncles kissed brides on their wedding day, but even to do that they pinned a dollar on the bride's dress. As far as I could tell, people didn't just give love away.

So imagine my surprise one summer day, during the hour that my parents were home for lunch, when I turned the corner from the kitchen to the living room and saw my father sitting in the large recliner we called dad's chair—although mom always sat in it—with my mother on his lap, kissing him! I thought I had walked onto a TV set. I must have stared, but mom didn't stop. What had happened? Had my father let her win the previous night's wrestling match? Were these aliens impersonating my parents? That sort of thing happened a lot on TV, like *My Favorite Martian*.[3] Or had we become Italian? Who knew?

My father had received an inventory bonus at the store. I immediately needed that information translated. What was a bonus? It meant we were going to get the swing set at Sears out of layaway. I wanted to kiss my father, but mom was hogging him.

Let's move on to that other great, misunderstood love. The Trinity is a difficult doctrine, because no adequate picture of the concept comes to mind. We know intuitively that an old man with a white beard plus Jesus and a bird is really quite inadequate, but we can't find a better image.

When I think of Trinity, I like to think of dad in that recliner and mom sitting on his lap kissing him. I can't claim credit for the idea. St. Augustine first suggested it when he likened the Most Holy Trinity to love, which is always tripartite, involving a Lover, a

Beloved, and the Love they share.[4] You don't have love without that trinity, and St. Augustine was simply echoing the New Testament teaching that God is love (1 John 4:8).

When Christians say "God is love," we mean more than simply that God commands us to love, or that God approves of love. The doctrine of the Trinity teaches us that the deepest reality we've ever experienced, love, is quite simply the deepest reality there is. Ultimately the universe itself is about love, because God, in God's own self, is love. It's like this: There is a Lover, the one we acknowledge as Father; and a Beloved, the one we call Son; and finally the Love they share, the one we name the Spirit. Or come at it like this: God did not need to create anything in order to love. God loved even when God alone existed.

To know love is to know God. This is why even the nonbeliever, who spurns our admittedly inadequate images of God, to the extent that he or she believes in love, opens the self to love, desires to plunge into the deepest depths of love, knows God and participates in God's own life and being.

In a way, this mystery of the Trinity puts us in our place. Love doesn't begin or end with us. A child with good parents may think the world revolves around him or her, because seemingly all of the parents' time and attention is given over to the child. But it detracts nothing from the love a child receives from his or her parents to know that their love existed before the child came to be, to learn that he or she is the fruit of love. One could say that the doctrine of the Trinity puts us in our place, and what a wonderful place it is! We came forth from love, a love so fruitful and free it pours itself out into creation.

There are so many days when life seems more effort than enjoyment, when sorrows seem greater than solace, when joy itself seems jostled out. That's when I think of that recliner, my father holding my mother, my mother kissing my father, because that's when I learned the mystery of the universe and the heart of the Catholic faith. And what I say of myself is true of you: I come forth from love. I was created to love. Love is my name and my home.

What Would Scarlett Do?

What comes to mind when you hear the name Scarlett O'Hara, one of the most memorable characters in American literature and film?[5] I think of the dresses, the hoop skirts, and the hats. I think of Tara, Twelve Oaks, and Atlanta burning. But who can separate Scarlett from the men she loved, the men she married, and, of course, the man she both loved and married? Just to recap, that would be the man she loved: Ashley Wilkes; the men she married: Charles Hamilton and Frank Kennedy; and the man she both loved and married: Rhett Butler. What can I say? Love is messy!

Scarlett is an *apparently* weak and frivolous girl (she sneaks out of nap time), but she grows into a very strong and determined woman. She saves Tara with ruthless decisions. But doesn't Scarlett remain in our imaginations because of the odyssey of her heart? Sometimes she simply ignores that heart. The girl marries Charles Hamilton on a whim; the woman marries Frank Kennedy to save her land. Yet if she generates sympathy, any feeling for her on our part, it's because she doesn't know her own heart. For so many years she thought that Ashley was the answer to every question, never asking the right questions, never seeing the love Rhett offered!

Stories don't become legends without telling us something deeply true about ourselves. So what do we see of ourselves in Scarlett's love for Rhett, a love that is confused, strong but abused, ever-present but diffused? Do we sometimes love like that?

The Scriptures speak the same way of our relationship with God, and they constantly remind us that we humans do not love with the same wholeheartedness as God does. From the book of Wisdom: "You have filled your children with good hope, because you give repentance for sins" (12:19). Sin can be defined as seeking something less than the whole, something disparate. From St. Paul's letter to the Romans: "And God, who searches the heart, knows what is the mind of the Spirit, because the Spirit intercedes for the saints according to the will of God" (8:27). The Spirit searches the heart, because the heart is not monolithic. It's divided within itself and needs the discernment of God. And remember the gospel parable of the wheat and weeds (Matt 13:24-30)? It's easy enough to cast ourselves in the parable's lead, as wheat, and then to fill out the cast of weeds with anyone we don't like, but the two parables that follow, the mustard seed and the leaven, complicate the plot (13:31-33). This gospel isn't simply a question about what parts of the world should be saved or damned. It's also about parts of us. It evokes what St. Thomas Aquinas would have called "concupiscence."

If you received religious instruction in the content-driven days, you learned that concupiscence meant a tendency toward sin. St. Thomas gave it a deeper meaning. He contrasted God who is whole, complete, and, one might say, utterly focused, with the human person who is disparate, disoriented, and dispersed within his or her own self. For St. Thomas, concupiscence, as the human condition, meant that we are still putting ourselves together. Like Scarlett, we don't yet know our hearts. We don't have the courage or wherewithal to make a complete gift of self to the one who loves us.

That's why we come to God again and again to offer ourselves. Unlike God, we can't do it once-for-all. We're still collecting ourselves. St. Thomas taught that as we pronounce our wedding vows, or promise lives of poverty, chastity, and obedience, we do so knowing that the gift we give will be fractured and incomplete, an imperfect expression of the heart, simply because the human heart is not yet complete. Thomas understood divorce, adultery, and clerical scandal. Yet he still insisted that humans must strive to love as God does, even knowing that we will sometimes fail. Why? Because a human heart set on anything less will lose the little humanity it has.

Like Scarlett, we grow, often painfully, usually with a lack of clarity, and almost never as fast as we should. Like Scarlett, the human heart is strong, but it's still finding itself, still gathering its own inner strength. The parable assures us that God is waiting to harvest the heart, to call it to himself. The dross will burn like chaff. What is wheat will make a worthy harvest. Meanwhile, God is eternal. God waits. You see, God doesn't need time to learn how to love well or deeply. But we do.

One Builds One's Own Jail

Though she had never met him, Katharine Hepburn insisted that Spencer Tracy play opposite her in the 1942 film *Woman of the Year*. In *The New Yorker,* Claudia Roth Pierpont writes that Hepburn's character Tess was very much the sort of gal America had always seen in the actress, "a woman immersed in a life of adventure and achievement and importance. In her relationship with Tracy—he's a sportswriter for the same paper—she's the intellectual force and the big success. Reversing all the clichés, it's he who gets upset when she's preoccupied with her work or fails to notice that he's bought a new hat."[6]

As many know, their off-screen romance was the opposite. Though Tracy never left his wife, Hepburn reoriented her career around his, suffering a nervous breakdown when he took up with Gene Tierney. Yet she nursed him through alcoholism, sometimes sleeping outside his locked hotel door until she could get inside to clean him up. She was still nursing him through the last five years of his life. Why? Why so much giving with so little in return? Perhaps Hepburn's answer is to be found in a definition of love she once offered: "It means I put you and your interest and your comfort ahead of my own."[7]

There are many—and they would have their point—who would say that Katharine Hepburn impaled herself upon Spencer Tracy, that she lost herself trying to find him. She simply said, "One builds one's own jail."[8]

The prophet Amos had to explain to the priest Amaziah that he never wanted to be a prophet; he was compelled by a word, and the force of the divine person behind it (7:14-15). Deep, authentic human life is always about being seized, about being compelled to respond, to love. Jesus sent his disciples to announce the reign of God. Like Judaism before it, and Islam after, Christianity presents itself as a revelation. In this case, it is ultimately the revelation of a person. Christianity insists that to know Jesus Christ is to find one's self. It insists that he is the very presence of God in our midst, the one who makes life comprehensible. It's quite a claim, that to know and to love Jesus is to find one's self, or conversely that to have missed this love is simply to have missed—love itself. St. John of the Cross wrote, "The strength and vehemence of love has this trait: Everything seems possible to it and it believes everyone is occupied as it is; it does not believe anyone could be employed in any other way or seek anyone other than Him Whom it seeks and loves."[9]

There are those who could never comprehend life pivoting upon one love, though that is the essence of Christianity. Perhaps then, they could also never understand Katharine Hepburn describing her tortured relationship with Spencer Tracy as "twenty-seven years together in what was to me absolute bliss."[10]

Desire of the Everlasting Hills

Brokeback Mountain, the movie based upon the short story by Annie Proulx that originally appeared in *The New Yorker,* became a cultural watershed.[11] There were cultural warriors, especially within the church, who immediately wanted to turn it into a topic for debate. Perhaps the tale is better considered as an opportunity for reflection. Either way, Proulx wrote a love story, and no one, not even the Catholic Church, says that love doesn't, or shouldn't, exist between two members of the same sex. Set aside genital expression for a moment and remember that love doesn't confine itself to the opposite sex. Even the church knows that. We've had too many saints who have deeply and chastely loved others of the same sex.

The powerful climax of Proulx's tale comes when Ennis discovers, years later in the boyhood closet of his deceased friend Jack, the shirts they wore the summer that they herded sheep together on Brokeback Mountain. Here's the passage from the original short story.

> The closet was a shallow cavity with a wooden rod braced across, a faded cretonne curtain on a string closing it off from the rest of the room. In the closet hung two pairs of jeans crease-ironed and folded neatly over wire hangers, on the floor a pair of worn packer boots he thought he remembered. At the north end of the closet a tiny jog

in the wall made a slight hiding place and here, stiff with long sus-
pension from a nail, hung a shirt. He lifted it off the nail. Jack's old
shirt from Brokeback days. The dried blood on the sleeve was his
own blood, a gushing nosebleed on the last afternoon on the mountain when Jack, in the contortionistic grappling and wrestling, had
slammed Ennis's nose hard with his knee. He had staunched the
blood which was everywhere, all over both of them, with his shirt-
sleeve, but the staunching hadn't held because Ennis had suddenly
swung from the deck and laid the ministering angel out in the wild
columbine, wings folded. The shirt seemed heavy until he saw there
was another shirt inside it, the sleeves carefully worked down inside
Jack's sleeves. It was his own plaid shirt, lost, he'd thought, long ago
in some damn laundry, his dirty shirt, the pocket ripped, buttons
missing, stolen by Jack and hidden here inside Jack's own shirt, the
pair like two skins, one inside the other, two in one. He pressed his
face into the fabric and breathed in slowly through his mouth and
nose, hoping for the faintest smoke and mountain sage and salty
sweet stink of Jack but there was no real scent, only the memory of
it, the imagined power of Brokeback Mountain of which nothing
was left but what he held in his hands.[12]

Ennis, clutching Jack's summer shirt, speaks to every heart.
Desire is so basic to human existence that one might use it as a
definition of what it means to be human. We simply are, every day
of our lives, a bundle of desires, hopes, longings. One might also
define God as that which finally satisfies human longing. The
church often brings Jesus before us in the figure of the bridegroom,
as the one who, in the beauty of his flesh, fulfills the prophecy of
Hosea: "I will now allure her, and bring her into the wilderness,
and speak tenderly to her" (2:14).

The Christian faith teaches that God, who is love, created us
for love. We were made, brought into existence, and fashioned in
every aspect of our being to respond to God. This means that desire
itself, the yearning we feel inside of us, is not merely an unsatisfied
and therefore disquieting aspect of our existence, but the very
manifestation of our orientation toward God, whom we define as
the fullness of life, of truth, of goodness, and of beauty.

In August 2002 one of the church's greatest living theologians gave a wonderful talk entitled, "The Beauty and Truth of Christ." The man, who was then Cardinal Ratzinger, began by quoting my favorite psalm, Psalm 45, "You are the most handsome of men; grace is poured upon your lips" (v. 2). He continued,

> Naturally, the Church reads this psalm as a poetic-prophetic representation of Christ's spousal relationship with his Church. She recognizes Christ as the fairest of men, the grace poured upon his lips points to the inner beauty of his words, the glory of his proclamation. So it is not merely the external beauty of the Redeemer's appearance that is glorified: rather, the beauty of Truth appears in him, the beauty of God himself who draws us to himself and, at the same time captures us with the wound of Love, the holy passion (*eros*), that enables us to go forth together, with and in the Church his Bride, to meet the Love who calls us.[13]

Whatever else it is, *Brokeback Mountain* is a story of love and desire. It's a tragic tale in which neither is allowed to come to fruition. It speaks to us, male or female, heterosexual or homosexual, married, unmarried, or celibate, because we have all known what it means to desire, to yearn without satisfaction. We may well be tempted to say, "That's life. It hurts and then we die." But the Gospel insists that our hearts are not heartlessly deceived. They were made for love; they yearn for love. If they remain open and persevere, they will someday know the fullness of love.

Joseph Ratzinger quotes a fourteenth-century Byzantine theologian, Nicholas Cabasilas, who puts it beautifully: "When men have a longing so great that it surpasses human nature and eagerly desire and are able to accomplish things beyond human thought, it is the Bridegroom who has smitten them with this longing. It is he who has sent a ray of his beauty into their eyes. The greatness of the wound already shows the arrow which has struck home, the longing indicates who has inflicted the wound."[14] Perhaps another way of saying this would be to suggest that no one can love us like love itself, the one whom we call Jesus. Of course human loves are not just way stations on the path to Christ, but the desire that remains within us even in their midst suggests that only God can truly satiate the human heart.

Maybe the church doesn't need *Brokeback Mountain* to teach her about love, but perhaps she could use the reminder. It's true that human loves can be disordered. They can deceive. It takes prayer and time to know which of them lead to God, but every love, even when marred by sin—as all our love is—still proclaims that we are destined, as we pray in the litany of the Sacred Heart, to love the "Heart of Jesus, desire of the everlasting hills."

Love among the Stars

As he remembered it, "The door opened not on the expected fan magazine version of a starlet, but on a small, slender young lady with dark hair and a wide-spaced pair of hazel eyes that looked right at you and made you look back. Don't get ahead of me: bells didn't ring or skyrockets explode, although I think perhaps they did. It was just that I had buried the part of me where such things happen so deep, I couldn't hear them."[15]

Remembering the same night, she would recall his invitation to dinner in order to discuss her "problem," noting that he had an early appointment the next morning. She responded by saying that the dinner was short notice and that she also had an early call. "I didn't, of course, but a girl has to have some pride. . . . Two hours later, my first thought when I opened the door was, This is *wonderful*. He looks as good in person as he does on the screen."[16] It was Ronald Reagan's first date with Nancy Davis, the woman the world would come to think of as "his Nancy."

Their motives were mixed. Nancy wasn't looking for a handsome star; she needed Reagan's help as president of the Screen Actor's Guild, because she had been blacklisted as a Communist sympathizer. Reagan himself was simply doing his best to cope with renewed bachelorhood. He was a year and a half out of his marriage with Jane Wyman, drinking too much, spending too much, dating too much, "a succession of actresses, singers, and models, including Patricia Neal, Ann Southern, and Ruth Roman."[17] His nightclub bills alone were running $750 a month. But, by a twist of fate, or the grace of God, one could say that both of these people stood in the door that night with their savior, though obviously it took time for that realization to dawn.

Saint Augustine taught that human beings were made for love, that we cannot possibly *not* love. As he saw it, even in base loves something of love's truth prevails. Reflecting on his youth he wrote: "So I arrived in Carthage, where the din of scandalous love-affairs raged cauldron-like around me. I was not yet in love, but I was enamored with the idea of love, and so deep within me was my need that I hated myself for the sluggishness of my desires. *In love with loving,* I was casting about for something to love."[18]

In one sermon he insisted, "There is no one of course who does not love, but the question is what do they love? We are not urged not to love, but to choose what we love."[19] Love is an enrichment of being; it completes the self. As Augustine saw it, human love doesn't compete with divine love, but it must be rediscovered, illumined, intensified in the love of God. He prayed, "For anyone who loves something else along with you, but does not love it for your sake, loves you less. O love, ever burning, never extinguished, O Charity, my God, set me on fire!"[20]

Unlike Qoheleth in Ecclesiastes 1:2—"Vanity of vanities, says the Teacher, vanity of vanities! All is vanity"—St. Paul is not negative about earthly life and its loves. Like Augustine, he simply asks that we allow grace to direct our love ever higher. "So if you have been raised with Christ, seek the things that are above, where Christ is, seated at the right hand of God" (Col 3:1).

Nancy Davis went to Hollywood, because she wanted to be a star. In her early years there she was often seen in the company of Benny Thau, the casting director for MGM whose casting couch was supposedly the busiest in Hollywood.[21] What was she really, deep down, looking for in Hollywood? What are we seeking in our lives?

It took Ronald Reagan two marriages to get it right. Yet in the end, Ronnie and Nancy found and chose each other, and I suspect that God has judged both of them as kindly as history itself. They might have looked for love in a lot of wrong places, but when it did come they responded to the call to come higher, to store their riches someplace better than this passing world.

St. Augustine would say that they simply allowed love to ascend. Nancy would say in 1997, when her husband was in the early stages of Alzheimer's, "Thank God we found each other. Our relationship was—is—unique. We were—are—very much in love."[22]

4

Suffering

Trusting the Script

Scripted

I had been ordained about a month when I received my first emergency call late one afternoon. The hospital said that a young man, age nineteen, had been crushed under the thresher of a wheat combine. My first thought was to find the pastor, since my seminary education in Rome had been quite long on theory and very short on practice. The presumption had been that our pastors would teach us the day-to-day work of a priest. Unfortunately, my pastor was away the evening the call came. I was it!

At least I knew where to find the oils. My sister had wisely recommended keeping them, along with the ritual book, in my car's glove box. She and my mother enjoy a quip about my not being able to find my head if it weren't attached. I raced to the hospital, finding the correct page as I drove. I had no image of what was to come.

A nurse was waiting for me at the emergency room door. "This way, Father." I was rushed by the boy's family, who burst into tears as I passed. I got the point. It had to be very bad if they had called for the priest.

I was completely unprepared for the bustle of the emergency room. It seemed to me like a TV set, except that an entirely naked young man, purple with large bruises all over his torso, lay on the table. Doctors were screaming commands; nurses were flying. I hugged the wall, afraid that someone would tell me to get out of the way, to get out of the room. A nurse came over to me. Into my ear she whispered stoically, "Father, you had better do what you've come here to do, because I can tell you now that what we're doing isn't going to work."

Eight years of seminary education, and I froze. The only way I could move was by telling myself: "You've seen the movies. What would a priest do? You've got to *act* like a priest."

I went over to the young man, whom I presumed was comatose. I stood at his head. It was the only spot free. I was sure that the doctors would tell me to get out of the way. Instead they worked around me, as though I were a fellow worker. I took the young man's hand and leaned into his ear. I told him that I was about to give him absolution. If he was sorry for his sins, he should squeeze my hand. He did, ever so slightly but unmistakably. I said the words of absolution, telling myself that Bing Crosby would not break down and cry.

I went on to anoint him on the forehead and hands, fumbling with the vial of oil. I made a cross with a dab of oil on his forehead, saying, "Through this holy anointing may the Lord in his love and mercy help you with the grace of the Holy Spirit." I reached down to anoint his hands. They were bruised and filled with needles. I put the oil on the back of his hands, too afraid to turn over his palms as I had been taught. "May the Lord who frees you from sin save you and raise you up."

I didn't understand most of the commands filling the room, but I could sense when they lost their urgency. The energy of the doctors simply deflated. There was nothing more they could do. My voice didn't break until I said the prayer of Final Commendation, the prayer we say when we know it's over. Even with Bing at my side, I could barely voice the words.

> Go forth Christian soul, from this world in the name of God the almighty Father, who created you, in the name of Jesus Christ, Son

of the living God, who suffered for you, in the name of the Holy Spirit who was poured out upon you, go forth faithful Christian. May you live in peace this day, may your home be with God in Zion, with Mary, the virgin Mother of God, with Joseph, and all the angels and saints.

I went out to be with the family. They had all gathered. It's what you do when someone you love is suffering. His father and his older brothers couldn't sit down. His sisters were with his mother, a large, muscular farm wife, her blond hair graying. She was quietly crying, bearing a cross that filled me with as much horror as that boy's bruises. I do not come from a demonstrative family, but—still using the persona of a movie priest—I put my arm around her shoulders. I didn't have much to say, so I listened as she looked into her apron, telling me about the accident and about her wonderful boy, about the blessing he had always been to her.

A few moments later, the doctor entered to say that they had "lost him." He knelt before the mother, told her that he was sorry they couldn't have done more. The damage had been too great. He rose and looked about. How limited his skill and power seemed when he proffered, "Would anyone like a sedative? No? Then I'll leave you to Father." He must have said more than that, though his words still seem powerfully brief in my memory.

One of the boy's sisters fell to the floor. She was down there, wailing with a force that terrified me. I couldn't understand why her husband didn't go to her. So I did. I got down on my knees and held her shoulders. Again, it seemed the role to play.

A short time later, the mother asked to say the rosary. We went to the hospital chapel and did so. People then began to scatter, to make phone calls, to pick up kids. No one can stare at death for long and not blink.

The book of Wisdom speaks of the just one suffering at the hands of his enemies. "If the righteous man is God's child, he will help him, and will deliver him from the hand of his adversaries" (2:18). It's a simple, forthright conclusion: a good God would not allow the just to suffer. Yet the gospels record Jesus bluntly teaching that "the Son of Man is to be betrayed into human hands, and they will kill him" (Mark 9:31).

All monotheistic religions face a common paradox drawn from one fact and two premises: the fact is human suffering. The two premises are the power of God and the goodness of God. How do these three go together? Some limit the power of God, saying that God allows suffering because God can't stop it. Others reject belief in any goodness greater than ourselves, saying that suffering exists because there is no God.

Christianity insists that in the cross of Jesus Christ a different truth has been revealed. In one way God is not all-powerful, in the sense that he cannot contradict his own meaning. God cannot take away evil. It is the result of our free choice for, or against, God, who is our very name for goodness.

And yet goodness *is* God; it is all-powerful and does have the last word, because, at the cross of Jesus Christ, God does what we do in the face of suffering. God makes our pain his own. God draws it into his own self and transforms it. The cross reveals the radical compassion of God. Like any lover, like that young man's family, God will *be there* to suffer with the beloved. In the end, *being there* is what matters most in human life, and in death.

As they left the hospital, I promised the family that I would come by the house in the evening. I remember walking to my car, exhausted. I sat down behind the wheel, closed the door, put my head on the steering wheel and wailed, much like that boy's sister. I cried a long time for someone whom I had never known. I'd not seen that in the movies. It was unscripted. It was God's gift, the grace of compassion.

Staying on Your Feet

As St. Mark tells the story, "many were coming and going." The apostles and Jesus "had no leisure even to eat." And so the Master sensibly told his apostles, "Come away to a deserted place all by yourselves and rest a while." Yet as "he went ashore, he saw a great crowd; and he had compassion for them, because they were like sheep without a shepherd; and he began to teach them many things" (Mark 6:30-34). If one listens with sympathy, one might even feel the burning in our savior's feet, the dryness in his eyes, the soreness in his shoulders.

What does it take to stay on your feet, to keep giving when you're depleted? Are we born with those reserves, or do we find them in the course of life? I'm inclined toward the latter view. Here's why.

I like college students (being priest and professor would be a poor choice of profession if I didn't). I like their optimism, even their cockiness. I often envy the sheer number of possibilities that lie before them. How wonderful to look out and see seemingly endless loves and adventures waiting for you! But I find that young people often lack an important quality of the more mature: perseverance. Maybe that has to grow with life itself. I find that young people are rather quick to surrender. If a door slams shut, they often fail to knock, much less shove. Perhaps with that vista of seemingly endless possibilities, they're not so compelled to stand their ground.

Woody Allen once quipped, "Seventy percent of success in life is just showing up." I would add that often what matters most is simply going on when you have every reason to give up, refusing to stop even though time seems to have run out or the diagnosis offered leaves little room for dispute. Sometimes it's simply a question of staying on your feet, like our savior.

Consider the year Sheryl Crow had in 2006. The svelte blond singer entered it having sold thirty million CDs worldwide and garnered nine Grammys. In 2006 she'd reach her forty-fourth birthday but, as she noted, "Forty is the new twenty."[1] Evidently! I saw the *Vanity Fair* photo spread. The year 2006 was also supposed to be the year when her famous engagement to Lance Armstrong, ten years her junior and seven-time winner of the Tour de France, would culminate in marriage.

But as Frank DiGiacomo wrote in *Vanity Fair*:

The couple never did set a date for their wedding, and today Crow remembers the winter of 2006 by a series of dates that made February the cruelest month of her life so far: On February 3, she and Armstrong announced in a joint statement that they were splitting up. On February 8, she attended the Grammys, where she was up for three awards and served as a presenter; (sic) but after braving media hordes still chewing over the break-up, she went home empty-handed. On February 11, she turned forty-four and marked the occasion with her band, who can be quite a bunch of cutups, at her home in L.A. Five days later, she went for a routine mammogram.[2]

On February 20, Sheryl Crow learned that she had Stage I cancer in her left breast. "But what follows is no sob story." DiGiacomo insists:

> The diagnosis changed her life irrevocably, Crow says, but it also brought perspective and clarity. Painful as her breakup with Armstrong was—and continues to be—and as much as she wanted him by her side as she faced her treatment and what lay beyond, Crow soon realized that even her heartbreak had to take a backseat to her healing. And once she got her head around that, she says, it pared away a lot of unnecessary baggage from her life.[3]

Sometimes the most important thing to do in life is simply to stay on your feet, to give no ground, even if you're not winning. Always athletic, Crow doubled her fitness regimen, giving up "Fritos, sugar, and her beloved breakfast of doughnuts or 'cheesy omelets.' She now starts the day with something called Simply Fiber and otherwise exists on what she labels an 'Eskimo diet,' rich in fish, herbs, and colorful vegetables."[4] She took up sand dune climbing and "stand-up paddle, a difficult-sounding activity that involves standing on a twelve-foot surfboard and propelling oneself with a long double paddle—a sort of vertical form of kayaking. Crow also read a lot, meditated, and had her horse Sally shipped west."[5]

Of course, response can also be over-reaction. But Crow seems to have faced her fears and found real wisdom. DiGiacomo writes:

She feels differently about her body since her treatment. Prior to her diagnosis, "my body was a demonstration in how not to look forty. There was a lot of ego attached to it, and I had to let go of all that. Because, literally, for eight weeks, I was sleeping a lot of the day," due to her surgery, a lumpectomy, and the subsequent radiation treatments. The fatigue was unsettling, because it did not mesh with her 24–7 Taking Care of Business work ethic. And so she gave into it, saying, "O.K., I'm going to let go of everything that is familiar to me." That included "being a fitness queen and a touring, working, recording artist." Making room for her treatment, "introduced me to a whole aspect of life," she says, which is: "When there's nothing to do, do nothing."[6]

Woody Allen is surely right. So much of life is simply about showing up. Our Lord continued to be shepherd, even when that meant being a weary shepherd. In October 2006, Sheryl Crow started touring again. Before that she'd busied herself writing a new album. Her father back in Missouri used to say, "Show me a loser and I'll show you a loser," suggesting that we really do choose more of our fate than we like to admit.[7]

According to Crow, "[T]he bottom line is all these events, these small or these huge catastrophic events in your life—I do think that that's where you really meet yourself. And then your life never looks or feels the same again. And it can only be better."[8] Our Lord let the crowds come. He embraced the wood of the cross. Small or catastrophic, he stayed on his feet. He just kept standing. Often, that's all that matters.

Offstage Mother

Her first husband abandoned her five years into their marriage, leaving her with two small boys. And by age twenty-five, the Dutch Baroness Ella van Heemstra was again pregnant and facing the dissolution of her second marriage. As much as we might covet them, titles don't pay the bills, and neither did her second husband, the unborn child's father, Joseph Ruston. "They had been married for three years; during that entire time, she reckoned that he had not worked a total of three months."⁹ The second marriage failed, but Ella's two sons and her third child, a daughter, survived its breakup, and the Second World War, in occupied Holland.

> [The daughter] could always rely on her mother's care, protection and instruction, but . . . Ella was not given to overt displays of affection. A Victorian baroness to her fingertips, she was now more than ever restrained, having lost the spontaneity and gaiety of her youth. She was a serious mother who always had her daughter's best interests at heart, but the warmth of that heart was cooled by her conviction that dignity forestalled cuddling, and that anything more effusive than a perfunctory good-night kiss was indecorous. . . .
>
> [And so the little girl] often wept in secret, for if she did so in the presence of others, she was scolded. "As a child, I was taught that it was bad manners to bring attention to yourself, and to never, *ever* make a spectacle of yourself. . . I always hear my mother's voice, saying, 'Be on time,' and 'Remember to think of others first,' and 'Don't talk a lot about yourself. You are not interesting. It's the others who matter.'"¹⁰

Everyone who came to know Ella's daughter, which is virtually the entire civilized world, would grant that the Baroness had turned out a proper lady, yet few ever realized how maternal distance had emotionally impoverished Audrey. Cary Grant once told her, "You've got to learn to like yourself a little more."¹¹

Whatever else one can say of the Baroness, she was always there for Audrey. At least that part of her that could be. It was Ella who sacrificed, working as a hotel clerk, a florist, a decorator, and a nanny, so that her daughter could attend a respected school of dance in London, which would lead to her being cast as a chorus dancer in musicals. The only thing Audrey received from her absent father was a name, and that was slightly ambiguous. Thinking his maternal descent more illustrious than the paternal, he had changed the family name from Ruston to Hepburn.

By the age of twenty-two, Audrey Hepburn had become a Broadway sensation in *Gigi,* but, as Donald Spoto records in his biography *Enchantment*: "The Baroness arrived on December 19, attended a performance of the play, went backstage, smiled and hugged her daughter for the cameras—and, typically, offered no praise. Indeed, her remark can hardly have been what Audrey expected or needed at the moment: 'You've done very well, my dear, considering that you have no talent.'"[12]

Is it possible to be present but not really there? To be someone without enough emotional support and love for another to make a difference in that person's life? Legitimate question for any child, and I think one raised by the farewell discourse of Jesus in the Gospel of John: "Do not let your hearts be troubled, and do not let them be afraid. You heard me say to you, 'I am going away, and I am coming to you.' If you loved me, you would rejoice that I am going to the Father, because the Father is greater than I" (John 14:27-28).

Hasn't every Christian, at one time or another, asked if it really had to be that way? Did Jesus have to withdraw from the world? Why not remain inside the world as its Lord? Why leave us apparently to fend for ourselves? One of the best answers to that question comes from the French philosopher Michel de Certeau, who wrote: "The Christian language begins with the disappearance of its 'author.' That is to say that Jesus *effaces himself* to give faithful witness to the Father who authorizes him, and to 'give rise' to different but faithful communities, which he makes possible. There is a close bond between the absence of Jesus (dead and not present) and the birth of the Christian language (objective and faithful testimony of his survival)."[13]

As Certeau sees it, truly foundational, soul-changing sagas only become so with the *absence* of their authors. As long as the founder remains, the limitations of time and space stand fast, but when someone withdraws, the work of symbolic imagination begins, allowing the very meaning of a life to expand. As odd as it sounds, for Certeau Christianity is fruitful precisely because Christ is absent, because in our longing for him we constantly recreate and newly envision him.

One could say that Christ withdraws to make room for the church. We could not grow into our own selves without his absence. There are those today who like to say, "Jesus yes; church no," but that's a profound misunderstanding of Christ and his mission. He comes not that we would cling to him, but that we might grow into ourselves because of him. Isn't that the way true love always works? Doesn't it desire the growth and goodness of the one loved? Christ comes so that we might be church, the Holy City of Jerusalem. "Christ loved the church and gave himself up for her" (Eph 5:25).

If the church doesn't seem worthy of our love, could we possibly be caught in a dangerous form of self-loathing, adoring an absent Christ while spurning the new creation, the church, which his Holy Spirit births? Granted, there is much in the church not to love. She is ever in need of reform. But to fail to love the church is to spurn the very love of Christ poured into the world. I am not thinking of pontiffs and hierarchies. Those are skeletal. You have to look to the pews to see the Bride's face and flesh.

We often define the church as the presence of Christ upon earth, but of course it's also the very manifestation of his absence. If Christ were immediately present to us, there would be no reason for the church. And yet the church isn't just a stand-in for Christ. It's his manner of both being present and withdrawing, so that we, and our fellows in the church, can become ourselves in the church, in him.

Suffering is similar. However one answers those age-old questions—Why does God allow us to suffer? or Where is God in the suffering?—one has to say that something happens to us in suffering, something that literally forms us, something that can only occur with the apparent withdrawal of God.

Leonard Gershe wrote the screenplay for *Funny Face* and in the process befriended both Audrey and her mother. He recalled that the baroness

> had a great sense of humor and so did Audrey. But unfortunately, they didn't have it together—they didn't share laughs. I adored her

mother, but Audrey didn't like her very much. . . . Ella played the role of stern mother. She was a different person when she talked about Audrey—judgmental—and she took her role of baroness quite seriously. On the other hand, Ella could be very silly when she wanted to be, and so could Audrey. But Audrey never knew that woman. They didn't know they were really very alike.[14]

What's the right distance for love? And make no mistake, it does require a distance! Too close, and the other is lost, drowned in one's own needs and projections. Too far, and the life-giving fruitfulness of love is lost. Ella stood too far back; in contrast, some parents smother. Ella did believe her daughter was a wonderful actress, but, according to Gershe: "She couldn't tell her that. Audrey once told me that she never felt loved by her mother, but Ella did love her, believe me. Often people can't tell the object of their love that they love them; they'll tell other people instead."[15]

Love is all about finding the right distance. We know that in word and deed, Christ has opened his heart. If he withdraws, seems absent, it is not for lack of love. It is to create the space his bride needs simply to be herself.

Jen Finally Talks

There are more than thirty thousand verses in the Bible. Makes you wonder why any of them stand out, like an old friend who is glad to see you again, but for me this one from Jeremiah (given here in the NAB translation) always does: "You duped me, O LORD, and I let myself be duped; you were too strong for me, and you triumphed" (20:7). The prophet utters these words just after being released from the stocks, where he'd been placed for faithfully proclaiming God's word. It's no wonder that he feels duped. In the ancient world gods entered into contractual relationships with humans. One honored the god in cult and expected blessings in return. To most minds in the ancient world, Jeremiah's imprisonment would mean either that Jeremiah's God was impotent or spurning him. Jeremiah could ask what kind of lowdown, lying god he has that he gets suffering for his service. However, Jeremiah responds to his imprisonment in a different way. He affirms that God is in control of events and that God loves him, despite the fact that he allows him to suffer.

Jeremiah's God is our own, which is why his words ring true. Who hasn't measured the distance between what one hoped of life and what one received? Who hasn't looked for blessings and found bruises? Some would call that the measure of maturation.

I rarely confess to reading the articles in *Vanity Fair*. I usually just look at the pictures, but how could I resist a cover with the headline: "Jen Finally Talks! And talks and talks. And cries. And talks." A lead-in was also on the cover: "Am I lonely? Upset? Confused? Yes. But I'm a tough cookie. . . I never said I didn't want to have children. I did and I do and I will."[16] I knew that I had to be there for Jen. I had to hear her story.

I'm not here to bad-mouth Brad. I know Jen wouldn't want that, and when it comes to bad mouths, to my mind that's what he's already chosen, those pouty lips included! But I do think Jen experienced her own Jeremiah moment, when the promise of God, of life itself, seemed hollow. From the article:

> "There are many stages of grief," she says. "It's sad, something coming to an end. It cracks you open, in a way—cracks you open to feeling. When you try to avoid the pain, it creates greater pain. I'm a human being, having a human experience in front of the world. I wish it weren't in front of the world. I try really hard to rise above it."
>
> Aniston is struggling to find a deeper meaning in the debacle. "I have to think there's some reason I have called this into my life," she says. "I have to believe that—otherwise it's just cruel."[17]

Jesus said to his disciples, "If any want to become my followers, let them deny themselves and take up their cross and follow me. For those who want to save their life will lose it, and those who lose their life for my sake will find it" (Matt 16:24). It would seem that the god, or life itself, that Jeremiah and Jen find—and Jesus preaches— seems almost to relish suffering. But can that be right?

Is God cruel? Count all the tears shed by humans and then argue that God isn't! Our faith, however, insists that suffering is not of God. It comes from the absence of God, from a willful rejection of God on the part of humanity. It's a sucking vacuum that entered this world when we first severed our union with God. Our faith also teaches that Jesus drew into himself the emptiness of evil when he mounted the wood of the cross.

Jesus never knew a moment of life that was not in communion with his Father, unless one counts the moment of his death, when the only bond between them was his naked and dying desire to do the Father's will. In that terrible moment of emptiness, when he allowed his life to be drained of everything save hope, I think he saw the world with a clarity that you and I will never know. Paradoxically, the smaller we become, the more we truly see the world. I think Jesus saw a world in pain and tasted its tears as he hung over the dark abyss created by our breach from God. When his lips drew their last breath, the very Spirit of God breathed again into the world.

The gospel says his death is a pattern destined to repeat itself until the last tear is shed. Somehow in the hollow pain of emptiness, we find life. When pain swells shut our eyes, and we can no longer look upon this world, the hope of another begins to breathe into us. It asks only our perseverance, our hope.

Here's how Jen explains it.

> It's sort of like Bambi—like you're trying to learn how to walk. You're a little awkward: you stumble a bit. The things you would do with your partner, you don't do. It's uncharted territory, but I think it's good for me to be a solo person right now. You're forced to re-discover yourself and take it to another level. If you can find a way to see the glass half full, these are the moments when you learn the most. I've had to reintroduce myself to myself in a way that's different.[18]

To say that something must die in order for life to go on is an expression of ancient, and weary, fatalism. To say that embracing the death we find in the middle of life is the path to eternal life is the hope of the Gospel. Jeremiah suffered long before Jesus, Jen well after, but a Christian reads both stories with the conviction that God's power is revealed in suffering because God's solidarity with us is made manifest in the Son who took his stance by our side and freely chose to suffer.

Who Remains When the Curtain Falls?

Missing another is a terrible sort of suffering, but perhaps looking inside your heart and finding something essential missing is even worse. I was recently looking under "T" for Trinity and came upon Tallulah, as in Tallulah Bankhead. Few people now alive remember her stage performances, and she didn't make all that many movies. Today she's usually characterized by her signature "dah-ling." Her voice was said to be "steeped as deep in sex as the human voice can go without drowning." Robert Gottlieb, writing in *The New Yorker*, called her "a star more than an actress, a personality more than a star, a celebrity before the phenomenon of celebrity had been identified."[19] She was all that, but the question one has when reviewing her biography is when, if ever, she was truly happy.

Her family in Alabama wasn't rich, though it was aristocratic and well placed. Tallulah's mother died of complications following her birth; her father Will collapsed into alcoholism. Gottlieb writes, "Even as a little girl, Tallulah was crazy to perform, and frequently when Will, somewhat the worse for drink, drifted home with his pals, he would lift her onto the dining-room table and have her entertain the boys with risqué songs. She reveled in it. A plump child with startling gold hair, Tallulah was an exhibitionist from the beginning."[20]

At fifteen she convinced her family that she was born to be an actress. They sent her to New York, where she lived with her aunt at the Algonquin Hotel. As she put it, "I was consumed by a fever to be famous, even infamous."[21] But something else was eating her insides. New York introduced her to alcohol, cocaine, and seemingly endless love affairs, the first with the actress Eva LaGalliene. Endless love affairs suggest an itch for something more than an affair, a hunger present, albeit in varying degrees, within each of us.

It was London's West End, however, that made her a star of the stage. She appeared there in sixteen plays. Gottlieb writes, "With her glorious hair, her unique voice and accent, her unrestrained dancing and cartwheeling (during her English career, she cartwheeled whenever the script allowed, and sometimes when it didn't) she did indeed conquer the West End."[22]

Hollywood brought her home. Her husky, seductive voice seemed created for the new medium of talking pictures. "In a year and a half, Bankhead made six feature films (and a lot of money) but none of them really worked. . . . The reality was that she was first and always a creature of the stage, all about projecting her larger-than-life personality at an audience, never about allowing a camera to explore her face and reveal her feelings. The movies caged and suppressed her."[23]

Tallulah lost a vigorous campaign to play Scarlett O'Hara in *Gone with the Wind,* but she redeemed her career on Broadway with her performance as a malevolent Southern matron in Lillian Hellman's *The Little Foxes.* A month after its opening, in March of 1939, she was on the cover of *Life.*

Back to that other topic under the Ts. I've never relished preaching the Trinity. For that matter, I've never relished preaching, but what's one to say about a doctrine which is defined as a mystery exceeding comprehension? One might go on about all that we don't know, but that seems less useful than discussing Tallulah Bankhead. I always believed that if doctrines don't make a difference in real life, they needn't be doctrines. So what does the Trinity do for me, and what might it do for you?

The doctrine that God is Trinity tells me that the terrible empty space in my middle doesn't belong there, that it doesn't have the last word. What terrible empty space in the middle? Of course, if we all shared the same space, it wouldn't be empty, but I'll do what I can to describe it.

It's looking at yourself with disappointment in the morning mirror. What were you thinking? That this was the day someone else would show up? It's checking your e-mails more times in an hour than one should do in a day, hoping that something in them will change everything. It's having a drink at the end of the day to wash it all away. It's looking at your spouse, your chosen one, and constantly remembering the one you didn't choose. It's going to a coffee shop because you can't meet people if you stay at home alone and then discovering that you feel more alone at the coffee shop than you did at home. It's loving your children so much that it hurts and yet being unable to enter their silence. Why can't you communicate with the only absolutely pure love you've ever known? It's wondering who you will be, who will be there for you, when your mother dies.

Or let Robert Gottlieb describe that terrible empty space inside Tallulah:

> As she passed the age of fifty, Tallulah's demons grew stronger. She had always been a heavy drinker; now she was consuming a quart of bourbon a day, together with a dangerous mixture of Tuinal, Benzedrine, Dexedrine, Dexamyl, and morphine. She had always been an insomniac; now she was frantic for sleep—as far back as 1948 she had been observed knocking back five Seconals and a brandy chaser after a night of drinking. She couldn't bear to be alone: friends, colleagues, servants, and the young men she attached to her and whom she called her "caddies" would be wheedled or ordered to sit on her bed (or lie in her bed) all night while she struggled for sleep.
>
> For years, she had said that she wanted to die. Once, playing the Truth Game with Tennessee Williams, she confessed, "I'm fifty-four, and I wish always, always, for death. I've always wanted death. Nothing else do I want more." It was a dozen years later, in 1968, that she finally got her way, quickly succumbing to double pneumonia. Her last words were "codeine—bourbon."[24]

It's a fundamental fact about human hearts: they weren't created to stand empty. If they don't find love, they will always look for something to dull the ache. How sad that Tallulah died trying to still the sorrow.

"For God so loved the world that he gave his only Son, so that everyone who believes in him may not perish but may have eternal life" (John 3:16). That's where our insight into the depths of the Trinity begins, with the face of the Son. We only know God to be triune because we became convinced that Jesus was God. Yet he spoke to God as his Father and promised to send God as his Spirit.

Whatever else, the Trinity tells me that the terrible space inside me does not exist in God. God is one, but God is also a *dialogue* of love. Love goes out of itself within God and finds perfect, fruitful fulfillment. The Father loves the Son and their love, as we say, breathes forth the Spirit. If love is the highest reality that we know as humans, then the doctrine of the Trinity tells us that God has never been without love, that God did not need to create us in order to know love, that God simply is love.

God is love. Notice that it's not "God commands love," or even that "God loves." It is simply: God is love. That terrible empty space within me, within you, is not of God. It is not our origin or our destiny. God is love. God is the one without an empty space.

When strangers on the street would inquire, "Aren't you Tallulah Bankhead?" she would reply with self-deprecating humor, "I'm what's left of her, darling."[25] Sometimes that empty space within keeps growing until what surrounds it is only a thin rind of self. Maybe then we're finally ready to be filled with the love of God, with the God who is love.

5

Christ

Myths, Movies, and the Man

Kind of Symbolic

Lucille Ball was three years old when her father died. She would later describe her life as a slow liberation from dependence upon men. Why? Because she had allowed father-substitutes to dominate her. For example, she registered as a Communist Party member to please her grandfather. She married a Cuban, one who continues to charm the world in reruns, yet Lucy's marriage to Desi Arnaz was marked from the beginning by her undue dependence upon his decisions, his abuse of alcohol, and his affairs with other women.

When trouble came, the couple tried to save the marriage. They worked less and traveled together more. They consulted a marriage counselor. Lucy even sought the help of Dr. Norman Vincent Peale, but Desi couldn't change. The issue was whether Lucy could outgrow her dependence upon father figures and step out of a marriage that couldn't work.

In his biography of her, *Ball of Fire,* Stefan Kanfer records that on a trip to Hawaii, "the couple argued for much of the time, and once, to cool off, Desi took a dip in the Pacific. He body-surfed for awhile and emerged minus a glittering gold chain that held a St.

Christopher medal and his wedding ring. Lucy was to categorize this as 'kind of symbolic. Our marriage was gone—so why shouldn't his ring be, too?'"[1]

Once, in preparing to discuss the historical evidence for the resurrection of Christ, I asked my class of college students how many of the Christians considered themselves to be true believers. They overwhelmingly did so. I then asked how many believed that Christ rose from the dead. What I was surprised to discover was that many did not believe that Jesus of Nazareth had ever existed. Obviously, I had a lot of history to teach, but what I find interesting is that the majority still believed in Jesus, but as a symbol, not a historical person. For them the story of Jesus was what anthropologists and religious scholars call a "myth," a symbolic story that offers meaning to life. It didn't have to be true. It only had to be profound.

But the church claims to celebrate history, not myth. It's true that the ancient world offered abundant stories of gods who died only to return again to life. These stories are myths, examples of human needs projected onto the divine, especially the need to overcome death itself. The idea is that, if the gods have already faced our fears, it's easier for us to follow.

What distinguishes the story of Jesus is that it is not about the death of a god who returns to life. It is about the death of a man, a convicted criminal who dies a terrible death. In the myths of the ancient world, gods entered death and returned. In this story, Jesus dies a man; he returns a God. I mean that the followers of Jesus watched a human being die, and they wept bitter tears. They had no comforting myth to explain the deed. It was brutal, full of hate, common and cruel.

Only the resurrection would transform the cross from the madness of the world to the wisdom of God. Centuries removed from the event, I admit that the story can sound mythic, but here's one reason to consider it more than a symbol.

Myths help men and women to sustain life, to soldier on; they do not fundamentally transform them. A myth cannot explain the radical change in the followers of Jesus. By their own admission, they had been afraid to die with him. Three days later they were risking death in preaching his resurrection.

The ancients used myths to console themselves in the face of death, but the apostles preached an event that provoked their violent deaths, deaths they embraced with a confidence born of truth. Myths only function when we don't know their origins, when those are clouded in times past and primordial. Would the apostles have been willing to die to create a myth? Who would die for what one knows to be a lie?

Everyone needs symbols, myths that help us to explain and comprehend our world. The question is whether we fashion our own or draw them from reality itself. The church insists that hers are woven in history, not imagination.

After her divorce, Lucy would soften toward Desi. Was life without him better than what she had known with him? During one such time

> a retired couple came backstage and introduced themselves. Instead of wanting an autograph, they had something to give Lucy. During a recent vacation to Hawaii they came across an object shining in the sand. "The lady opened her purse and pulled out a gold chain with a Saint Christopher medal and a wedding ring," Lucy told a friend. "I looked at the ring and it read, 'To Desi with love from Lucy.' I thanked them, kissed them both, and then closed the door and wept. Just closed the door and wept. It's funny, but it was then that I knew it was really over. Having that ring in my hands didn't bring the good times back to me, it brought the terrible times back, and I knew it was right. I knew Desi and I could be friends, but that we shouldn't be married."[2]

Many people live their entire lives without questioning the myths and symbols that order and offer meaning to those lives, but growth comes when we candidly examine what we believe and why we believe it.

Perhaps there is an additional question worth asking. Why do I believe? It might take some time, but another question will demand even more: How is my life different because I believe?

The Sopranos Sign Off

Speaking of mythic men, doesn't Tony Soprano come to mind? I resisted the lure of HBO's *The Sopranos* for the longest time, telling those who would ask that I didn't find mobsters all that interesting and wasn't drawn toward violent entertainment, but several years into the series, with accolades for excellence mounting, I finally broke down and rented the first season.[3]

I still remember the first episode of *The Sopranos*. It seemed more suburban comedy of manners than gangster saga. Tony rather awkwardly chased down someone who owed him money, first in his Mercedes and then on foot, eventually pummeling the man. I guess that's when I made the same concession that virtually every character in the series made. I could live with a little violence for the sake of the family. And like everyone else, viewers and characters, I became more and more attached to *la famiglia* and more immured to the mounting violence.

On June 10, 2007, I joined millions of Americans to watch the series finale. In ending, the show was true to itself. Watching it, one was always expecting violence, and nothing would happen. And then, not expecting violence, everything would happen. That was the genius of the show, which is why the last seconds continued to captivate. We knew that anything could have happened.

By now the entire world knows that Tony, his wife Carmela, and his son A. J. sit down to dinner in a New Jersey dive. Tony's daughter Meadow is outside, parking the car. It appears that there is an armistice in the war between the New York and Northern New Jersey crime families, and yet the camera keeps cutting from Tony's family at the table to sinister looking characters around them. Is this Tony's Last Supper? Will we learn that sin eventually delivers its scourge? Or will the Sopranos simply continue to live the way they always have, literally selling their souls for the suburban dream?

Meadow finishes parking the car and races toward the door of the restaurant. Will she see her family slaughtered? Or sit down to supper? We never know, because, as she pushes open the door, the screen goes black. The series is finished, and America either derides or celebrates the genius of *The Sopranos*'s creator David Chase.

One of the most perceptive reactions to the finale came a week later in the "Week in Review" section of *The New York Times,* when the author Charles McGrath compared the series to other pieces of literature whose endings are incomplete. He wrote, "In 'The Sense of an Ending,' a classic text of literary theory, the critic Frank Kermode says we crave endings for the same reason that some religious sects look forward to the Apocalypse—because it's the ending that gives shape and meaning to the otherwise random events that precede it."[4]

I think that's absolutely true, and true of more than just some religious sects. I think it's built into the human mind to seek and find order and meaning. Science allows us to impose those upon nature, but history seems to resist any such ordering. Christianity insists that history is eminently purposeful, but that its ultimate meaning will be revealed only in the final revelation of the Christ.

Here I think the would-be atheist is more at a loss than the believer. Atheists might spurn what they consider to be the simple answers of religions, but they aren't truly able to escape the essential human desire for meaning and purpose. We want history, the world's and our own, to mean something. We can settle for not knowing what it means now, provided we have some assurance that seemingly disparate strands of history will be pulled together eventually, like a masterpiece of literature where every scene, every character, every twist of plot seems purposeful in light of the denouement.

Consider the figure of St. John the Baptist. We've learned so quickly to associate him with the Christ that it's possible to miss seeing him for himself. Scholars tell us that he was an apocalyptic preacher, convinced that God was ready to intervene radically in human history. He insisted upon moral conversion to ready humanity for what was about to happen. Ultimately, he didn't attract the world's notice. Outside the New Testament, only the

Jewish historian Josephus mentions him. In the scheme of world history, the crowds weren't that large, the conversions didn't create a clatter. He was arrested for what today would pass as political agitation, and the gospels record that he lost his life on the whim of a woman and the weakness of a monarch. Left to himself, John would have passed into the impenetrable silence of history.

Of course, he didn't. He didn't because the Christ came to him for baptism, because the Christ embossed his ministry with his own. We call him the forerunner, because he was taken up into the constellation of the Christ. The early church could thus explain his significance with the lapidary formula, put into the mouth of Jesus himself: "Truly I tell you, among those born of women no one has arisen greater than John the Baptist; yet the least in the kingdom of heaven is greater than he" (Matt 11:11).

Quite a historical claim. If one heeds it, it brings to prominence the essential claim of Christianity: that all of human history has found its purpose, its explanation, and its focus in Jesus of Nazareth.

Think about our own lives and their ultimate meaning. Like untold billions who have gone before us, most of us will pass out of history without a trace. And realize just how quickly that will happen. Most people can't even give the names of their great-grandparents.

If that's true, what do we want to say that it was all about? Will death simply sever our existence, like a television screen going black, or will the threads of hope and faith that we call our lives be drawn up into the person of the Savior? What we say of John the Baptist we say of ourselves: life finds meaning and purpose in relationship to the Christ.

The Sopranos signed off the same way that so many of the characters lived their lives. Who could say what it all meant? There were always loose ends in the show. Plot lines proliferated and weren't always properly pegged down, at least for those who want conclusions. Remember the Russian gangster, shot and bleeding, running away in the snow? We never know what became of him. And through it all, Tony Soprano was always shrugging and saying, "Whaddya gonna do?" One could say it was his own lapidary way of denying the purposefulness of life. At least David Chase got us to question our own facile ways of defining life's meaning. Scholars use the word "myth" to indicate a story so foundational, so epic, that it creates meaning itself for those who tell it. But people in the street use the word to designate something false, bogus. The paradox is that one could ascribe the word to Tony Soprano in the first sense, only to realize that in the end it's the second that registers.

There are those who write off the story of Christ as mythic in the illusory sense, but try finding a larger myth in which to dwell. Can a story that speaks life itself be an illusion? Even tombstone inscriptions, those great final declarations of purpose, fade. For a Christian, the only question worth asking is whether or not these words will as well: "And this is the will of him who sent me, that I should lose nothing of all that he has given me, but raise it up on the last day" (John 6:39).

Death and the Other

One criticism of Mel Gibson's *The Passion of the Christ* was that the film focused excessively upon the passion of the Christ. Seems an odd criticism given the movie's title, but the critics were suggesting that the film didn't tell us very much about the significance of the man who died. In other words, we get the death but not the life. Gibson could reply that, if nothing else, he offered truth in packaging. He might also, if he had a philosophical or literary bent, mention Heidegger and Hemingway.

The German existentialist philosopher taught that death is a leavening agent for life. Martin Heidegger compared human beings to arrows. From the moment of our birth, we are aimed toward death. The arrow never veers off course, never slows its pace. We may spend our lives trying to forget that fact, but Heidegger suggested that authentic human existence begins when we face our own mortality: I am going to die. All of my projects will cease. I do not have unlimited days with which to remake my life. Knowing that, what do I want that life to be about? For Heidegger, death sharpens life. We create a limited masterpiece, because every masterpiece must be limited.

Gibson might also cite Ernest Hemingway, who suggested that a man's death says everything about his life. I consciously use the noun "man," because Hemingway was obsessed with the question of masculinity. He penned a short story about the death of Christ that is much like Mel Gibson's movie. Hemingway's Christ is a man's man, because he suffers more than other men could endure.

So perhaps Mel Gibson could say that we learn all we need to know about the life of the man simply by watching his death. He would be in good company if he did. Saint Mark's gospel is constructed around what scholars call "the Messianic secret." No one in the gospel story except the demons knows the true identity of Jesus, not even his disciples, who keep getting it wrong. The human being who finally understands and professes his identity is an outsider, the Roman centurion who watches him die, watches how he dies, and says, "Truly this man was God's Son!" (Mark 15:39). Mark is also suggesting that death has a way of throwing revelatory relief back onto life.

But let me introduce a third thinker, the Jewish philosopher Emmanuel Levinas. Levinas disagreed with Heidegger about death. It doesn't bring life into focus, he said. On the contrary, death is the great darkness before which the light of the human intellect fails. We cannot look behind death; we cannot look beyond death. Death is totally "other" than us. Levinas argued that human reason cannot say that death extends life or extinguishes it; reason must simply fall silent before that which utterly confounds it. All we know is that death is absolutely other than us, than life.

After this minicourse in the philosophy of death, imagine the thoughts of St. Peter during those hours between Good Friday and Easter Sunday! Everything he knew and loved about the man was gone. We talk about memory and meaning living on, but memory and meaning fade with the eventual death of survivors. Anyone can write on a tombstone, "We will never forget you!" But no one destined for the darkness of death can keep that promise. What did the death of Jesus mean to Peter?

Now, try to enter the mind of Peter when Jesus is restored to him. What is death in the light of resurrection? Who is the Christ, come forth from the tomb? Light is an apt image, especially because this light blinds in its sheer intensity. In the dazzling light of resurrection, does death focus life? Does it still confound life? Does the way in which one dies follow one into eternity?

Peter isn't given the opportunity to question the one who defies death. Jesus questions him, repeatedly: "Do you love me?" Odd question for a man back from death, and it's followed by an odd command: "Feed my lambs" (John 21:15). What is John teaching us?

I find Levinas helpful in answering this question. He suggests that human beings really become human when they find themselves before another human face and realize that this face makes infinite demands. Levinas says that if death is impenetrable, so too is the human face. We may frequently think that we know the other, especially those closest to us. Levinas insists that we are always wrong. Whatever we know is nothing compared to that which we do not know. When we realize that the other infinitely exceeds our capacity to comprehend, only one response is worthy of human life: absolute respect, deference, kindness. We can never calculate the value of the face before us; we must therefore treat it as priceless. Life finds its meaning and its dignity in my reverence for the face standing there before me.

Peter must have had so many questions. Who wouldn't want to query the one who returns from death? Instead, the face he loves directs his eyes to the others who will depend upon him, his faith, and his strength: "Feed my lambs."

Peter will live out his days in a way Heidegger would admire. He knows what his life is about. He will die in a manly way, one Hemingway would envy, crucified upside down. But most of all he will live for others in a way that gives meaning to the Lord's prophecy about him in the Gospel of Luke: "But I have prayed for you that your own faith may not fail; and you, when once you have turned back, strengthen your brothers" (22:32).

Human, Divine, or Both?

Frequently, though admittedly to little effect, I warn students to be wary of information found on the Web. I always say that consulting the Internet is like reading restroom graffiti. Some of what you peruse might well be true, but a lot isn't. And speaking of restroom scrawling, in like manner, Dan Brown's research for *The Da Vinci Code* seems like that of a promising but lazy undergraduate. He often finds good material, though he doesn't read far enough to get it right. Consider this passage from the novel. Don't worry if you don't know the characters. They're no more developed than those of a Warner Brothers cartoon. Lee Teabing, an "expert" in the Holy Grail and everything else an afternoon of Web surfing might yield, explains to a gullible young French woman named Sophie the role that the Emperor Constantine played in divinizing Jesus Christ. He supposedly did this by suppressing the gospels we now call Gnostic.

> "More than *eighty* gospels were considered for the New Testament, and yet only a relative few were chosen for inclusion—Matthew, Mark, Luke, and John among them."
> "Who chose which gospels to include?" Sophie asked.
> "Aha!" Teabing burst in with enthusiasm. "The fundamental irony of Christianity! The Bible, as we know it today, was collated by the pagan Roman emperor Constantine the Great. . . . To rewrite the history books, Constantine knew he would need a bold stroke. From this sprang the most profound moment in Christian history. . . . Constantine commissioned and financed a new Bible, which omitted those gospels that spoke of Christ's *human* traits, and embellished those gospels that made Him godlike. The earlier gospels were outlawed, gathered up, and burned."[5]

I get paid to teach undergraduates how many falsehoods there are in those paragraphs. In this context, let me mention only a few. Count all the gospels you like—accepted, banned, and burned—and you won't arrive at eighty. You won't get beyond the teens. And Constantine had nothing to do with the selection of New Testament material. The list of accepted books was settled long before he converted to Christianity.

The worst whopper of the paragraph is the claim that the gospels Constantine suppressed emphasized the *humanity* of Jesus! He needed to do this in the novel to hitch Jesus to Mary Magdalene, but one wonders if Dan Brown has ever read a Gnostic gospel. They don't preach a human Jesus.

Gnosticism was a syncretic movement that predated Christianity, and threatened Judaism as well. The word *gnosis* is Greek for knowledge. We call them Gnostics because, although they thought themselves to be faithful Jews or Christians, they taught a secret knowledge to initiates.

What was the secret? Essentially that the world where you and I live is evil simply because it is material. According to Gnosticism the world of flesh and blood in which we live is the creation of a malign half-god, not the unknown God of pure spirit, who didn't create anything. That God dwells in unapproachable light. Everything else simply emanated down from him with the goal of someday finding its way back. One could say that, according to Gnosticism, inside each of us a fragment of God is trying to phone home.

Perhaps the fundamentals of Gnosticism sound good to you: knowledge liberates you, and the knowledge setting you free is that you don't really need anyone else. You're already "simply divine." One doesn't have to talk about sin or redemption. Many intellectuals today, Harold Bloom at Yale, Elaine Pagels at Princeton, proudly call themselves Gnostics. Gnosticism teaches that each of us is a God waiting to happen, so why not celebrate that fact rather than seek forgiveness from a putative savior and his church? And we do know that some primitive Gnostic communities allowed women greater leadership. So it's easy to see why Gnosticism gets a second chance among intellectuals. But feminism deserves better than Gnosticism, and intellectuals don't become well paid without putting their finger on America's pulse.

Then why did early Christian bishops ban the Gnostics and accuse them of subverting the Good News of Jesus Christ? You needn't look further than the gospels we've always had.

> He said to them, "Why are you frightened, and why do doubts arise in your hearts? Look at my hands and my feet; see that it is I myself. Touch me and see; for a ghost does not have flesh and bones as you see that I have." And when he had said this, he showed them his hands and his feet. While in their joy they were disbelieving and still wondering, he said to them, "Have you anything here to eat?" They gave him a piece of broiled fish, and he took it and ate in their presence (Luke 24:38-43).

The Christ proclaimed by the church, a church that quickly took to calling itself Catholic to distinguish itself from the countless sects that inevitably arose, is not a spirit come to save us from the world, as he is in Gnosticism. He is God incarnate in the flesh, who comes to draw creation, material and spiritual, into his own divinity. In Gnosticism Jesus is a teacher saving us *from* the world. In Christianity he is a savior not from but *for* the world.

Luke goes to great pains to show that the resurrection is not a purely spiritual event. Our flesh, our material world, our environment, has been raised by Christ to a higher realm. Early in his pontificate, Pope Benedict XVI suggested that one can compare the resurrection of Jesus Christ to an evolutionary leap. In Christ's resurrection the world itself has sprung forward.

Gnosticism, like many forms of Eastern spirituality, views this world as something to be escaped, cast off. Christianity sees this world, the one revealed to us anew in the very flesh of Jesus Christ, as worthy of reverence, precisely because it has been taken into the flesh, into the very person of the Christ. That's why the sacred images that fill Catholic and Orthodox churches are drawn from the human. A person who knew nothing about our religion, looking about our churches, might conclude that we worshiped humanity itself, and he or she wouldn't exactly be wrong. Christianity can't be reduced to humanism, but it does celebrate the human precisely because our humanity, in Christ, has been made the channel of divinity itself.

Perhaps this is a good place to mention that the early Gnostics were more accepting of women because they considered them to be broken males, farther down the ladder of emanation, lacking the intellectual quality of men. In the world of pure spirit to come there would be no male or female, because women would be changed into purely spiritual males. In fact, sex wouldn't exist at all. But then neither would chocolate chip cookies or stars or sunsets. Thanks, but no thanks.

The irony is that many Christians naively carry about a picture of heaven that is virtually Gnostic. They think we're going to sit on clouds and play harps, but who would want such an ethereal heaven? No, heaven is this world redeemed and renewed! It's not a realm of pure spirit. If it helps, picture it with sex and chocolate chip cookies, stars and sunsets, because we proclaim the redemption and divinization of this creation, not its destruction. "Then I saw a new heaven and a new earth; for the first heaven and the first earth had passed away, and the sea was no more. And I saw the holy city, the new Jerusalem, coming down out of heaven from God, prepared as a bride adorned for her husband" (Rev 21:1-2).

Even liars sometimes speak the truth. Let me finish with one more passage from *The Da Vinci Code*:

> Teabing cleared his throat and declared, "The Bible did not arrive by fax from heaven."
>
> "I beg your pardon?"
>
> "The Bible is a product of *man*, my dear. Not of God. The Bible did not fall magically from the clouds."[6]

Dan Brown is accidentally right. Though the book portrays the Catholic Church as the great villain, it's fundamentalist Christians who should feel most threatened by *The Da Vinci Code*. Why?

Because a fundamentalist naively presumes that the Bible did fall from heaven and that somewhere along the line the Catholic Church became unfaithful to its teaching. Dan Brown forces Christians who want to defend their faith to confront early Christian history, and when one does that, one learns that the Catholic Church, in the persons of her evangelists, wrote the Scriptures in order to proclaim her Lord, and, in the persons of her bishops, the same church selected those writings that faithfully preached the Lord's Gospel, rejecting those that subverted it. The Bible did not arrive by fax. It is the living testament of a church that brought it into being to proclaim her Lord, a church that still faithfully guards the truths committed to her when Christ sent her forth to proclaim his Good News to the ends of the earth, an earth destined not for destruction but for consummation in the glory of God.

I Dream of Jeannie

One Wednesday in *The New York Times,* Alessandra Stanley reported on the fall television lineup, announcing that with "the collapse of the dot.com bubble, the shakiness of mega-media conglomerates, the corporate accounting fraud scandal and insider-trading charges," television executives had determined that American viewers were tired of reality.[7] So reality television was out and programs that make us forget were in.

Good news for me. I've never been a fan of reality television. I always say I get enough reality with life. When I turn on the tube, I want to be spirited away. I'm still eagerly awaiting a revamped *Family Affair* of my childhood. Life was better with Uncle Bill and Mr. French watching over us, and, since we're in a retro mood, why not bring back the character Larry Hagman made famous? No, not J. R. Ewing. Go way back to Major Anthony Nelson, the astronaut who found the bottle in the sand, the one that left him dreaming of Jeannie.

What I liked about the television of my childhood was how unlike my own life it was. Who wouldn't rather drink coconut juice with Ginger than go to school? Why couldn't I grow up and marry a witch like Samantha? Of course, some men may feel that's exactly what happened to them, but without the lovely Samantha part.

What I found a source of endless fascination about *I Dream of Jeannie*—besides who it was who might have decorated the interior of her bottle—was the need to limit her wish-granting power.[8] So many of those surreal sitcoms required a certain built-in limitation. Gilligan's crew couldn't leave their island, or there would be no story the following week. Hogan's heroes couldn't escape en masse, because then there would be no Stalag 13. Jed, Granny, Elly May and Jethro had resolutely to remain hillbillies through nine seasons, or there would be nothing to laugh at. Think of the challenge the writers of *I Dream of Jeannie* faced: they have a genie who can give you anything you want. How does one keep the plot within bounds? Remember this question: "If a genie could grant you one—and only one—wish, what would it be?" The answer always struck me as obvious. I'd wish for unlimited wishes! But if Jeannie granted every wish, there would be no story to tell, no narrow escapes from Colonel Alfred E. Bellows discovering everything. At first Major Roger Healey was on the wrong side of the secret, but when he found out about Jeannie, he had to become one of the conspirators. There always had to be a middle ground between desire and its fulfillment.

Saint Thomas Aquinas would have understood my wish for unlimited wishes. He once defined the human person as *quoddam modo omnia*.[9] It's a Latin phrase meaning, "in some way, everything." Aquinas spoke of the human being as the one creature on earth with unlimited desire, wishes without end, an inexhaustible need to know. As Aquinas saw it, and long before Gene Roddenberry dreamt of *Star Trek*, the entire universe is the object of our desire to know, to experience, and to love. We exist "to boldly go where no one has gone before." One could say that it is humanity's collective vocation. We simply are desire, endless desire for something more, and anything that would deflate our desires would have the same effect as cancelling a classic sitcom. We'd no longer be humans without our desires.

Wasn't Aquinas correct? Have you ever met a human being who said, "I do not need any more love," or "There is nothing more that I desire to know." Or how about this: "Thanks, but I've had quite enough of beauty!" Aquinas taught that to be human is ever to yearn, and he defined God as whatever it is that brings the human heart to rest. Another way of putting it would be to say that because human desire is unbounded, it can only be satisfied by that which knows no limit. That's why in Aquinas, even the beatific vision isn't static. We won't look on God and say, "Oh, so that's who you are." The sound we make will be closer to the ones made by folks on a roller coaster, something endlessly dynamic and thrilling.

But there is a flipside to the human capacity for infinite wonder and unbounded desire. Sometimes it feels more like a restless heart and a bottomless pit. Yearning can be both delightful and depressing. If we, like Solomon, could ask God for anything and know our request would be granted (1 Kgs 3:5), would we choose wisdom? Would we want to remain on the journey, to stay open to what would come, to be able to discern in everything that comes our way something still sweeter, something yet deeper?

Aquinas did not define sin as choosing something evil, because in the end all is of God and evil itself only a privation, a lack of God. Humans sin when they stagnate, when they find the object of one small wish and squeeze the thing until it dies. We try to make the finite into the infinite. Sin is the refusal to yearn, to hope, and to wonder.

"The kingdom of heaven is like treasure hidden in a field, which someone found and hid; then in his joy he goes and sells all that he has and buys that field. Again, the kingdom of heaven is like a merchant in search of fine pearls; on finding one pearl of great value, he went and sold all that he had and bought it" (Matt 13:44-46). Wait a minute! The kingdom of God is about grasping? How can that be? Whenever you don't understand the kingdom of God, look at Jesus, who is that kingdom in the flesh.

You know Jesus when you come to understand what Paul tells the Romans: "We know that all things work together for good for

those who love God, who are called according to his purpose"
(8:28). ~~You need not grasp. You can hold your arms open, even to the wood of the cross.~~ You have found the pearl of great price. You have unearthed Jeannie's bottle. You can have all the wishes you want. Because you have set yourself free from that which is not of God, you are free for God. The great discovery is this: ~~We were given boundless hearts, because they alone can receive what is to come.~~

By the Grace of God

"Terry . . . Terry . . . Terry! Stop doodling and go to the blackboard. What's that all over your hand?"

"Eraser crumbs, Mrs. Ross."

"Well, wipe your hands—and NOT on your pants!"

"Now, all of you, outline along with Terry the following sentence. 'Mrs. Blake has three apples and a ham in her shopping cart.'"

"Mrs. Ross?"

"Yes."

"What part of speech is a Mrs.?"

"It's part of a proper noun. And in this case the proper noun is functioning as which part of the sentence?"

"Terry? Terry? Where is your mind? What part of the sentence is Mrs. Blake?"

How can I tell Mrs. Ross that my mind isn't at the blackboard? It is outside, in front of school. And what is my mind doing out there? It is watching a large, black limo pull up. A Bentley, though I wouldn't have known then what to call it. It is accompanied by several other cars. On the side of the Bentley is the Royal Insignia. A chauffeur exits on the right and holds open the back door for . . . Elizabeth the Second, by the Grace of God, of the United Kingdom of Great Britain and Northern Ireland and of Her Other Realms and Territories Queen, Head of the Commonwealth, Defender of the Faith.

What, you well may ask, is she doing in front of St. Joseph's Parochial School, Ellinwood, by the grace of God, Kansas? I'm glad you asked. It was all part of an elaborate scheme to have her first-born son grow up normal and unaffected by palace palaver. Charles is simply an actor, a stiff-backed ninny plucked straight from the pages of *Tiger Beat*. Her real son, the heir and future king, is a simple fifth grader, who at this very moment is humbly outlining sentences at the dusty blackboard of Mrs. Ross's classroom.

Mrs. Ross herself is momentarily startled by the commotion at the door of her classroom. "Make way for the Queen!" a Beef-eater barks.

But she has the good sense to drop to her fleshy knee, place her hand over her sagging, chalk-besmeared breast, and gasp, "Your Majesty."

"Mrs. Ross, we give you our right royal thanks for teaching this our beloved and, until now, hidden heir the principle parts of speech and their usages in the sentence. Your services are now concluded as it is our intention to return forthwith to Buckingham Palace with our royal son Terrance."

There's an audible gasp. It's not from Mrs. Ross. Somehow, she's always known. You just can't hide blue blood, not even beneath eraser crumbs. No, the gasp comes from Ellen Moeder, who realizes that she shouldn't have tattled on me for talking while Mrs. Ross was out of the room earlier in the day. For all Ellen knows, the rack awaits.

But I already have the mind of a prince and intend to begin my new royal life with largesse. Ellen will be pardoned. Mrs. Ross will be pensioned. The kindly grocer and his wife who have raised me will come to Balmoral Castle for summer visits. They can bring along my siblings, Harold and Bad Penny.

But all that can wait. In the meantime I have a question for my new mother. It's the same question I have often asked my former mom, but now I have good reason to expect an affirmative answer. As we make our way down the steps of St. Joseph's, I ask, "Mum, can I have a pony?"

The first temptation of the spiritual life is the refusal to engage life itself. It's the often unvoiced, but never silent, desire to live some other life in some other place in some other manner. Authentic spirituality is always an engagement with the real. While it does draw us toward what might be, it never bypasses what is. If God summons forth the world into existence, how can one engage God without engaging the world God created?

Our temptation is to fashion an alternative world where a God of our own design reigns. A book as poorly written as *The Da Vinci Code* would not enjoy the phenomenal success it did without tapping a vein. These days, who isn't prepared to believe the worst of the Catholic Church? Could there be a better climate to suggest that an elaborate, secret plot is in play at the Vatican? But the novel gives expression to something deeper than the zeitgeist. We have a perennial, innate desire for an alternative story. For centuries, Christians have heard these words from John's gospel and wondered if they didn't refer to a hidden revelation, to another, unknown audience: "I have other sheep that do not belong to this fold. I must bring them also, and they will listen to my voice. So there will be one flock, one shepherd" (John 10:16).

Read church history. We've never gone a century, not even a decade, without someone coming forth with the story of a vision, an apparition, a lost book, or a revelation given only to a few. But why do we want the story to have a hidden chapter? Why do we cry out with Peggy Lee, "Is that all there is?"

One could say that the struggle for secret knowledge dates back to Genesis. God sees all that God has created and declares it good. What is and what is known are one and the same, and they produce delight. Yet Adam and Eve can't help but wonder if something has been withheld, kept secret. Instead of delighting in the real, they seek power over it through arcane knowledge.

Genesis teaches that God made human beings to know, to desire. That's how we grow and become the very people we were meant to be in the eyes of God. To hunger for knowledge—knowledge of what matters, of what yields growth, of what will produce peace—is something a human being cannot cease doing.

But Genesis also suggests that this natural, God-given hunger for knowledge of the real was subverted by a novelty in human life, the ability to lie, deceive, and withhold. Henceforth human knowledge would have to mean not only delight in the real but also discernment of the false.

It is interesting that in the New Testament Satan is no longer simply the adversary that he is in the Hebrew Scriptures. There he is something of a mischievous imp, but in the New Testament he's called "the tempter," "the slanderer," "the enemy," "the liar," and "the angel of the bottomless pit."

Why? Why heighten the power and meaning of Satan? Because Satan was the converse of Christ, the darkness that ironically pointed to the light and power of Christ. Because Christians were convinced that what was given in the Christ was the ultimate Word of God, the complete expression of God's own being. At the beginning of his gospel, when John says that Jesus is the Word of God, he does not mean one possible word among many, not a word that God uses now only to discard later. Christians believe that Christ, as the Son of God, is the very act of God's self-expression. God never speaks a partial word; God never acts incompletely.

To St. John's early Christian community, asking if the Gospel of Jesus Christ is true, complete, and final, is only to show that one has not yet grasped what has been given in the Christ. John ends his gospel by solemnly declaring that everything needed has been revealed: "Now Jesus did many other signs in the presence of his disciples, which are not written in this book. But these are written so that you may come to believe that Jesus is the Messiah, the Son of God, and that through believing you may have life in his name" (20:30-31).[10]

Jesus is the great love letter of God. He cannot deceive, cannot be incomplete. The love of God has been encoded into his very flesh. This is why as Christians we do not, cannot, expect another. We don't look for "secret knowledge" because Jesus is the very self-expression of God. Everything we need to know has been expressed in him. The Christian who wonders if there isn't something more is a bit like a Kansas boy daydreaming about what simply isn't real.

Meanwhile, back in Kansas. This time the real Kansas. At three fifteen every day after school, a car would be waiting outside of St. Joseph's Parochial School. It contained a grocer, not a monarch. He was there to pick up three kids and take them home to await the arrival of their mother an hour and a half later. Each day he brought candy. Either three Cherry Mashes, three Reese's peanut butter cups, or, my favorite, three Hershey bars. I always thought that nothing says "I love you" more than a Bentley and the promise of a pony. So much self-deception built into human knowledge. To love and to ponder the real, to delight in its promise of what will be, is of God. To spurn what is in favor of fantasy is the bottomless pit the New Testament warns us against.

What says "I love you" is not the whimsy of imagination, a wish for what isn't. By the grace of God, it's not a Bentley. It's a Chevy Bel Aire and a Hershey bar.

6

Prayer

Going Straight to the Producer

Wizard

"Stop! I forbid you!" yelled Uncle Vernon in panic.

Aunt Petunia gave a gasp of horror.

"Ah, go boil yer heads, both of yeh," said Hagrid. "Harry—yer a wizard."

There was silence inside the hut. Only the sea and the whistling wind could be heard.

"I'm a *what*?" gasped Harry.

"A wizard, o' course," said Hagrid, sitting down on the sofa, which groaned and sank even lower, "an' a thumpin' good'un, I'd say, once yeh've been trained up a bit. With a mum an' dad like yours, what else would yeh be? An' I reckon it's abou' time yeh read yer letter."[1]

As you can see, some fantasies do come true. Don't take my word for it. Think of barren Hannah praying all that time, only to give birth to Samuel. Sarah laughed when she was told she would have a child. And who would have picked David for king? Peter for leader of the church? God likes to surprise. One might even go so far as to define God as "surprise," as that which constantly eludes and undermines our schemas and agendas. But back to Harry:

Harry stretched out his hand at last to take the yellowish envelope, addressed in emerald green to Mr. H. Potter. The Floor, Hut-on-the-Rock. The Sea. He pulled out the letter and read:

HOGWARTS SCHOOL
of WITCHCRAFT *and* WIZARDRY
Headmaster: Albus Dumbledore
(Order of Merlin, First Class, Grand Sorc., Chf. Warlock,
Supreme Mugwump, International Confed. of Wizards)

Dear Mr. Potter,

We are pleased to inform you that you have been accepted at Hogwarts School of Witchcraft and Wizardry. Please find enclosed a list of all necessary books and equipment.

Term begins on September 1. We await your owl by no later than July 31.

Yours Sincerely,
Minerva McGonagall
Deputy Headmistress[2]

And that was how Harry Potter joined a long list of legends who began life in the wrong life, that is to say, in a life other than the one they were destined to live. The theme is as old as literature itself, stretching from Harry at least as far back as Moses, who was raised as an Egyptian prince, not knowing his Hebrew identity. The list includes Heracles and King Arthur, the story of Cinderella and *The Princess Diaries,* and Pip of *Great Expectations.* And don't forget the Kansas boy—the one from Krypton—who isn't really the son of Ma and Pa Kent.

The story of a hidden, true identity is archetypal, expressing a deep conviction of the human spirit: the life we live isn't the life we are meant to lead. There's something missing, some identity yet to be revealed. One could say that we have yet to be introduced to our own real selves.

But even if we share the notion that a deeper, truer self has yet to be revealed, the question remains how that self is to be found. The answer begins with a basic human insight. How does anyone become who he or she is? Through relationships. We become who we are by interacting with those who share our lives. How does one find one's God-given identity? The same way: by the communion with God that we call prayer, in all its forms. Moses lifts his arms in prayer, and the battle belongs to Israel (Exod 17:8-13). Jesus taught us "to pray always and not to lose heart" (Luke 18:1). Why? It's difficult to understand the command to pray always without asking the purpose of prayer. Why do we pray?

We pray because we are in need. That's how I define the human person: that spot in creation constantly in need. Like Moses, there is always some struggle at hand, and so we look to God. Obviously we can comprehend the notion of an insufficient creature praying to an all-sufficient creator. There doesn't seem to be a culture that hasn't arrived at that notion of prayer. But is the purpose of prayer complete with petition? Is the work of prayer finished when our needs have been presented? What's the most important thing Major Nelson found in that bottle on that deserted island? A source of unlimited wishes or a new relationship that would change him and his world? He found a love that would change his place in the world.

The *Catechism* speaks of prayer as communion, and it quotes the youngest Doctor of the Church, St. Thérèse of Lisieux: "For me, prayer is a surge of the heart; it is a simple look turned toward heaven; it is a cry of recognition and of love, embracing both trial and joy."[3]

When human beings pray, they seek. Either within or without, they sense a presence, one seeking to communicate itself. Prayer is simply a human heart turned toward this presence. Someone is there, offering the self to us. In prayer we encounter God as the other, the one who matters most. Why? Because the revelation of that mysterious identity contains our own, still lost in mystery. In prayer we lose ourselves to find God. Ironically, we look for God to find ourselves.

When a person falls in love, that person realizes for the first time who he or she is. Why? Because the communion of authentic human love is always a communication of identity. Find the beloved and you find yourself, your place in the world, your deepest identity. You discover that you exist to love the beloved.

We tell stories of people like Harry, the misplaced wizard, because something tells us that we are misplaced, that we have yet to meet the one whose presence will reveal our own souls, who will make them shine with the luster of love. That's what we seek in prayer. To be in the presence of a love that reveals, because to look with eyes of love is to see not only the Beloved but our own true selves. St. Paul puts this beautifully when he writes: "All of us, with unveiled faces, seeing the glory of the Lord as though reflected in a mirror, are being transformed into the same image from one degree of glory to another" (2 Cor 3:18).

Gilligan's Island

I'd like to consider an American classic, a story of brave resistance against terrible odds, of a community forged by adversity, of the human spirit's boundless creativity. So

> just sit right back and you'll hear a tale,
> a tale of a fateful trip
> that started from this tropic port
> aboard this tiny ship.
>
> The mate was a mighty sailing man;
> the skipper brave and sure.
> Five passengers set sail that day
> for a three hour tour.[4]

Did you know that you can interchange the words and melodies of the theme song to *Gilligan's Island* and "Amazing Grace"? And you thought showbiz spirituality was just something I made up!

I grew up watching *Gilligan's Island*. I can't vividly remember its brief, three-season, prime-time run, but the plots became seared into my consciousness even before the rise of cable, because the show became a standard after-school TV offering. I was young

enough when first introduced to *Gilligan's Island* to accept its premise, and I tuned in daily, thinking this might be the episode when
the castaways were rescued. Schoolyard pundits of my day would
deliberate about how the latest scheme to get off the island had
almost worked and analyze what went wrong. None of us were
savvy enough to note that if they had been rescued we would have
had no more show to watch.

What I found fascinating about the show was the sheer fecun-
dity of life and invention those castaways managed to bring to that
tiny, deserted isle. If it was a three-hour trip, why did the Howells
have so many different outfits? I was amazed at the ingenuity of the
castaways. Who carved those coconut cups they were always using?
Where did Mary Ann bake those coconut cream pies on the island?
I took for granted that the professor was a PhD in everything. He
could repair anything, invent everything, and hold learned disputa-
tions on any known subject.

I fantasized about life as one of the castaways. I wanted so badly
to live in a grass hut with French doors and sleep in a hammock.
Would I grow up to marry Ginger or Mary Ann? Probably Mary
Ann. She was, after all, a castaway from Kansas! We'd have that in
common, and, even at seven, I knew that my driving skills would
probably never be able to negotiate Ginger's curves.

Remember St. Thomas Aquinas defining the human person as
quoddam modo omnia—in some ways, everything? He meant that
human nature, collectively and individually, is potentially ordered
toward the entire world. There is nothing that doesn't interest us,
nothing that doesn't draw us in. For Aquinas the human person
was the center of God's earthly creation, that spot where the world
itself became conscious and was drawn outward in search of the
other. Aquinas saw human life as the self-consciousness of creation
gathering up its knowledge and insight to turn lovingly toward the
God who had created it.

The problem is that we dissipate ourselves. Instead of being
drawn outward and upward, we turn this way and that. We dally.
We toil over that which is low, enervating, and vertiginous. Instead

of ascending a ladder of life-giving loves to the God who is their source, we wallow in self-love, self-interest, and spoilage of the self. We see the world and those who dwell within it as something to be mastered, controlled, possessed.

What amazed me about *Gilligan's Island* was that for all their creativity, beauty, intelligence, and industry (Remember the Howells' golf course on the island?) the castaways couldn't summon up their energies for the one thing needed. Whenever it came time to get off the island, they quarreled; they lied about how much baggage they were putting on the rescue boat; they dallied in division while the Russian cosmonauts were departing.

When Jonah enters Nineveh, the great city, preaching repentance, her citizens respond as one to repent and beg God's forgiveness (Jonah 3). Something within them tells them that their vital energies have been scattered. Wealth has not brought abundance. Jesus begins his public ministry and writes the opening score of salvation with the words: "The time is fulfilled, and the kingdom of God has come near; repent, and believe in the good news" (Mark 1:15).

Repentance is the Gospel portal, because only a change of heart, a redirecting of our desires, can summon up the vital energy that God gave to human life. When human life is dissipated, it grows flaccid. It begins to fester. Its vital energies remain, but they rot without outward movement. Sin is always a dissipation. St. John of the Cross insisted that sin produces a "dullness of mind and darkness of judgment in understanding truth and judging well of each thing as it is in itself."[5]

Søren Kierkegaard once defined a saint as someone who can will the one thing.[6] He correctly perceived that human life is a powerful vortex of energy. It's meant to draw all things into itself but then to direct that self toward completion in the other, ultimately in God. The saint subordinates everything to this passion. The sinner allows piddling passions to subjugate the self. The saint fills the world with life, because he or she seeks the fullness of life.

My generation has tried to recapture its childhood television memories, either in studio productions or made-for-TV movies.

Both attempts to resuscitate *Gilligan's Island* have failed, I suspect, because adults, even those trying to recapture their childhoods, can't buy the premise of the story. How could seven desperate castaways be so blind, so inept, so unable to summon the resolve and the energy to do what had to be done? Yet come judgment day that may well be the impression that comes over us as we watch our own lives in rerun.

You Know You're Getting Old When . . .

You know you're getting old when you tune into TV Land to watch *Green Acres* and Lisa Douglas, that Park Avenue matron from your childhood with the golden beehive hairdo and the stunning wardrobe, suddenly looks—well—hot.[7] You never noticed that as a kid and now feel like you're in some sort of Mrs. Robinson time warp. That's why I don't dare to tune in for *I Dream of Jeannie.* Can forty-something celibacy withstand Barbara Eden with her midriff exposed?

"Genie" is an Arabic word that we would translate as "spirit," because in the Arab world genies did what spirits are believed to do among all indigenous people: they explain the unexplained. Perhaps I should explain. Before the Greeks gave us our concept of nature, an orderly system following a pattern that can be studied and mastered, primitive peoples thought that events that we would now call acts of nature were the work of spirits—essentially hidden, capricious persons. Where does the wind come from? The spirit or god of the wind. The same was true of rain or fertility or sickness.

All languages and cultures have some expression for these apparently capricious acts. Think spirits, leprechauns, genies. Of course the monotheistic faith of Judaism and, following it, Christianity and Islam rejected the agency of such spirits. But they remain to an extent in the affirmation of angelic existence, although when Paul speaks of principalities and powers, he considers these spiritual creatures to be acting in accord with a well-ordered plan of God.

Yet something of the capriciousness of genies and spirits remains rooted in the use of the very word "spirit." When the Old Testament spoke of God's spirit, it clearly wanted to affirm the radical independence, transcendence—even capriciousness—of God's activity among us. The spirit is sovereign, subtle, acting in ways we cannot predict or even imagine.

Christians have found their imaginations stymied a bit when it comes to the Holy Spirit. We picture Jesus, probably incorrectly, as a pale man with a beard. We imagine God the Father of Jesus, absolutely incorrectly, as an old man with a beard. When it comes to the Holy Spirit, we're left with a dove or fire, two metaphors that were chosen somewhat capriciously, simply because they express capriciousness. A bird flies where it wills. Fire is contagious, fast, powerful, and unpredictable.

That's why it's difficult for the Christian imagination to warm up to the mystery of Pentecost. The feast celebrates the solemn promise and presence of the Holy Spirit, which is what ultimately makes all prayer fruitful. Without the Spirit, we would have no living bond to God, and certainly not to his Son, who would remain a figure locked in the past. With the Spirit, we know union with God. But how does one picture Pentecost? We can imagine a baby in a manger, something emotionally easy to digest. The same is true of the crucifixion. We understand suffering. Easter is more difficult. We can imagine an empty tomb, but resurrection remains harder to picture. By the time we arrive at Pentecost, the Christian imagination is depleted. We're asked to consider an aspect of God, and one of the divine persons of the Trinity, that remains beyond our ken.

Perhaps our consolation is that it must remain beyond our ken. We know the Spirit not by representation but by act, and we only know the latter after the event. The actions of the Holy Spirit are always unexpected, novel, and outside of any context.

The philosopher Martin Heidegger liked to speak of what he called the "event," that moment when the entire world changes. The event suffuses the world with new meaning. Think of falling in love, having a child, losing a job, hearing a terrible diagnosis. The event is never of our making. Instead of fitting into the world, when it comes it radically reconfigures the world.

That's one way to imagine the Spirit, as that which cannot be imagined, as the event that changes the world in an instant. We cannot imagine the Spirit, because the Spirit is the very capriciousness of God. If the Spirit of God belonged to this world, we would have an image, but the Spirit shatters all images in remaking the world.

That's why almost half a century later, Samantha Stephens and Major Nelson's Jeannie still enchant us. Why? Because they remake the world on their own terms. They take something mundane, the Latin-derived adjective for "world," and make of it something enchanted, a Latin-based word meaning "to sing." Think about it. Is there a better understanding of God's Spirit than that which enchants, which makes this old world sing?

Enterprise

There had been six U.S. naval vessels before her, each named *Enterprise*, but it would be the CV6, the sixth aircraft carrier built by the U.S. Navy, commissioned on May 12, 1938, that would guarantee the name "Enterprise" its indelible role in U.S. history. Because it was in the process of returning from Wake Island, the *Enterprise* barely missed the Japanese attack on Pearl Harbor. Had she been lost in that unexpected assault, the course of world history probably would have followed a widely variant vector. After that day, the CV6 *Enterprise* participated in every major battle in the Pacific, except that of the Coral Sea, when she was escorting the *Hornet* for the Doolittle Raid on Tokyo. In June of 1942 she played a crucial role in the Battle of Midway, where the course of the war was altered. Many times she held the line alone in the Pacific, becoming the most decorated ship in U.S. History. She earned 20 battle stars, sank 72 ships, and destroyed 911 planes.

Her successor ship, the first nuclear-powered aircraft carrier in the U.S. fleet, was launched in September 1960 as the longest, tallest, and mightiest warship ever to sail the seas. Shortly after noon on October 7, 2001, it was this *U.S.S. Enterprise,* the CVN 65, that launched America's military response in Afghanistan to the darkest event in American history, the September 11th attacks.

Yet, at home and around the world, even those who know nothing of U.S. military lore know the name *Enterprise,* because it has also served as the moniker for seven Federation starships of Gene Roddenberry's science fiction, multigenerational epic, *Star Trek.*[8] In September 2000, the fifth television series based upon Roddenbury's vision premiered. It was entitled simply *Enterprise.*[9]

Roddenberry's epic first aired in 1966, a time of worldwide crisis and tension when many thought humanity's future held little promise. Roddenberry wanted his fictional future world—a world where war, prejudice, and poverty itself had been banished—to be a harbinger of hope. It was an artistic statement of confidence in the future of America and the world. Several times in the weeks following September 11th, I turned off the news and turned on *Star Trek.* I suspect I was not alone. In times of crisis, fiction and fantasy become the home of hope.

The American Thanksgiving holiday always brings with it a plethora of platitudes about all that we have to be grateful for despite the times. However, few Christians know that the ancient Christian word for Jesus' memorial meal, *Eucharist,* means "thanksgiving." They are unaware that the Mass itself is based upon an even more ancient Jewish prayer of thanksgiving, the *Todah.* Nor do they know that the night before he died, Jesus led his followers in their faith's great act of thanksgiving, the Passover. Yet this is why Christianity proper has no feast of thanksgiving. It's because every Eucharist, celebrated every Sunday and virtually every day in some denominations, is the church's great act of thanksgiving.

Most Catholics were taught that the Mass is a sacrifice. Protestants were taught to speak of a single sacrifice, one performed by Jesus on the Mount of Calvary. Each approach is true enough as far as it goes, but the roots of the Christian Eucharist are, to quote the Jewish text Psalm 50, "the sacrifice of thanksgiving." We give thanks for Jesus, because Jesus taught us to do so.

On the night of September 11th, Americans of every faith and of no faith gathered to pray. Catholics came together to celebrate the Eucharist, literally and rather oddly, "to give thanks to God." The paradox may not have been apparent to many who do not know their own faith well, but it was as real as it was fundamental to that faith. Who can help but ask: what were we grateful for on that night, and why do we continue to give thanks?

One can always begin with the naive platitude that those of us who were praying were alive and therefore should simply have been grateful for that, but doesn't that immediately raise the question of offering thanks to a God who allowed so many others to die? So why did we offer thanks?

At every Eucharist, in the power of the Holy Spirit, we address the Father of Jesus Christ and thank God for having entered, and fundamentally changed, human history. If you will, Jesus Christ is our *Enterprise*. He is the great sign and promise that the future is ours, because we belong to God, who is the beginning and the end of human history. Whatever comes, we know that history belongs to God, and we acknowledge Jesus Christ to be the great turning point, the living Exodus, in the drama that is human history.

There is so much we don't know, so much to fear, but when Gene Roddenberry named his first fictional starship *Enterprise*, he wanted to suggest that humanity's future was full of hope. The best of the past would still bear fruit in days yet to come. In the end, Christians offer the Eucharist because of a geometrical calculation. Between one point and another there is only a straight line. We call Jesus Christ the alpha and the omega of human history. We offer thanks, because nothing can remove us from God's own trajectory.

Phantom Zone

Randy Barta was two years older than I, and when you're nine that's quite a bit older and a lot smarter! He lived across the alley, which is where, though you mustn't tell anyone, our secret clubhouse was located. It was underneath a pile of boxes in his father's steel storage shed.

When Randy and I weren't playing *The Man from Uncle* or running through the neighborhood with towels tied around our necks, as superheroes are wont to do, we would be in the clubhouse discussing whether a raccoon was smarter than a cat or even more weighty issues such as whether Superman would trounce Batman if they ever had to fight each other, say because Lex Luther or the Joker forced them into it. Randy actually believed that Batman would win, but then he also thought Marvel comics might be better than DC. Lord, deliver us from heresies!

It was Randy who first introduced me to the concept of the fourth dimension. It went something like this:

"You see everyone knows there are three dimensions: length, width, and height."

"Yeah . . . uh . . . everyone knows that, sure."

"But some scientists think there might be a fourth dimension?"

"Which scientists?"

"What do you mean, which scientists? Really smart scientists who study life on other planets; the guys who invented *Tang*."

"Oh, those guys."

"Exactly! See this fourth dimension might be right here, all around us, only we can't see it because we're three-dimensional creatures."

"You mean like the Phantom Zone where Superman had to exile General Zod, who was also from Krypton but used his superpowers under earth's yellow sun for evil rather than good?"

"Exactly! For all we know there are beings right here with us, right now, but we can't see or hear them."

"And later Superboy had to place his cousin Mon-el in the Phantom Zone, because he was allergic to lead rather than Kryptonite, and twentieth-century earth is full of lead, and Mon-el had to stay in the Phantom Zone until the twenty-third century when Braniac Five, a descendent of the original Braniac but good rather than evil, developed a serum that could allow Mon-el to leave the Zone and join the Legion of Super Heroes?"

"Yeah, like that, I'm telling you. There may be another world right here in Kansas. Maybe we're in that other world, or maybe our *evil twins* are."

"Of course, I say 'later' Superboy put Mon-el there, but really that was before Superman exiled General Zod there, because Superboy is Superman, only younger, so he came first in time."

"Enough with Mon-el! I'm saying do you realize that maybe only a thin veil separates us from the fourth dimension?"

"So how do we get to the other side?"

"How do we know we're not on the other side?"

"Then how do we get to the other, other side?"

"If I knew that, would I be wasting my time talking to you under these boxes?"

He had a point, and I think it's one worth remembering when we hear our Savior exclaim, "I thank you, Father, Lord of heaven and earth, because you have hidden these things from the wise and the intelligent and have revealed them to infants; yes, Father, for such was your gracious will" (Matt 11:25-26).

I'm not sure why it is, but as our conception of ourselves grows with experience and education, we tend to picture God as farther removed from our world. It wasn't always like that. Small children expect God to answer their prayers. When they ask their guardian angels to check under the bed for monsters, they have real confidence that the task is done, but as we grow older the God we picture is somehow more removed from us, dwelling at some future, distant point in the cosmos, less responsive to prayer, less involved in our daily lives. We think we do justice to the transcendence of God when what we've really done is to surrender something of God's immanence.

The Scriptures insist that God entered our world in Jesus Christ and that the Spirit of Christ still hovers over that world, breathing life into its tired lungs. As they see it, a very thin veil separates us from the other side. St. Paul tells the Romans, "But you are not in the flesh; you are in the Spirit, since the Spirit of God dwells in you" (Rom 8:9).

I don't think one can understand the Christian faith, certainly not Catholicism, if one pictures the world of the Spirit as loftily dwelling in some remote recess. The martyrs were convinced that they could almost touch another world, and that death would finally puncture the membrane separating them from the Beloved. In like manner, one can make no sense of celibacy if one imagines it to be only a sterile "no" rather than a breathless, anticipatory "yes." The sacraments come into their own when we think of them as portals into that which was and is yet to come.

When Jesus says, "Come to me," he cannot mean *across* the reaches of space and time. There must be a way for all that simply to part and for grace to flow. There must be another dimension as close to us as the one we see around us. Why is this so easy for children to understand and so difficult for adults to believe? Are they gullible, or have our eyes grown dim? Can we really enter this other, spiritual dimension with nothing more than an act of the will?

Join me under the altar. Well, at the altar. We'll talk.

Letting Be

According to his biographer, Donald Dewey, "Harry Truman said he would have made the perfect son, Natalie Wood said he would have made the perfect father, and Gloria Stewart said he *did* make a perfect husband."[10] So it would seem that the forthright, manly-yet-vulnerable, passionate-yet-wholesome Jimmy Stewart whom America discovered on the big screen bore considerable relationship to the man who lived on earth. But sometimes we might wonder where he came from. Who fathered Jimmy Stewart? Who reared his boy into such a man?

His name was Alex Stewart, the owner and proprietor of the Stewart Hardware Store in Indiana, Pennsylvania. "As his son once described it: 'The store was not only his method of making a living but his forum where he pronounced opinions seldom tailored to the popular style. If he had ever heard of the slogan about the customer always being right, he would have scorned it as toadyism as well as a falsehood. He constantly assured his customers, friends, and family that there was one correct way to do things—his way.'"[11] Sometimes, according to Eleanor Blair, that attitude cost him business:

> My mother-in-law never tired of talking about the time she went to the hardware store to buy some green paint. Alex, who had never seen the inside of her house, began telling her to pick another color, that green wasn't right for the walls she had in mind. My mother-in-law insisted that she wanted green. Alex insisted that she was being silly, and obviously didn't know very much about room decor. Finally, she just got tired of arguing and walked out. I don't think she ever went back, either. Alex had a habit of self-starting himself into arguments like that, and the more you argued back with him, the more he seemed to lose himself more deeply into what he was saying. If he hadn't believed what he had been saying at the beginning, he did by the time he was finished.[12]

Alex Stewart doesn't sound all that promising as father material, does he? One expects to hear of a son cowed by the demands of a domineering dad, but Alex Stewart possessed a paternal quality not unlike the mystery Christians celebrate in the Eucharist. He could practice what the German philosopher Martin Heidegger called *gelassenheit,* he could "let it be," as the Beatles once sang. True authority creates a space for liberty. It allows those who are subject to that authority enough room to be themselves. Alex Stewart the father knew when to step aside so that Jimmy Stewart the son could become his own man. The son remembers:

> When a neighbor's dog killed my dog, whose name was Bounce, I vowed to kill that dog in revenge. I vowed it day after day in the most bloodthirsty terms. I never quite did it, but I was making myself ill with my own hate and frustration. "You're determined to kill this dog?" my father demanded abruptly one evening after dinner. "All right, let's stop talking about it and get it done. Come on."
> I followed him to the store, to discover that he had tied the dog in the alley. He got a big deer rifle out of stock, handed it to me, then stepped back for me to do my bloody work. The dog and I

looked at each other. He wagged his tail, and his large brown eyes were innocent and trusting. Suddenly the gun was too heavy for me to hold, and it dropped to the ground. The dog came up and licked my hand.

The three of us walked home together, the dog gamboling in front. No word was ever said about what had happened. None was needed. Dad had taught me I wasn't really a killer, and I didn't have ever again to try to work it up or pretend. It was a great relief.[13]

Yes, Alex Stewart engineered his son's discovery of mercy, but he didn't produce it. He let it come forward of its own accord. One could say he stood back enough to let Jimmy become Jimmy.

Now consider the *gelassenheit* of God, God's own letting be. Every religion understands what it means to worship a deity, to honor a mystery larger than ourselves. In that sense, there is something filial about all forms of religious life: we acknowledge a power greater than ourselves, asking of it forbearance and blessing. But what other religion suggests that the deity whom it worships humbles himself enough to die upon a cross, or to give himself into the hands of his adherents, as Christ does in the Eucharist?

We often try to ponder the awesome mystery that we celebrate at every Eucharist. We should also contemplate the wondrous "letting be." The God who allowed himself to dwell in the womb of the Virgin, who humbled himself to die upon the cross, the God whom earth and sky cannot contain, humbly rests in our hands and feeds our flesh with his own. The old hymn puts it beautifully:

Panis angelicus
Fit panis hominum;
Dat panis coelicus
Figuris terminum:
O res mirabilis!
Manducat Dominum
Pauper, servus et humilis.

The bread of the angels becomes the bread of man;
the bread of heaven is given a bounded form.

O wondrous thing! The poor, the slave
and the humble man feed on their lord.

In this sacrament God lays aside, lets be, the prerogatives of divinity
so that our humanity might flourish. How wonderfully paternal,
in the best sense of that word.

> At one point, when he was ten, [Jimmy] Stewart was so obsessed
> with animals that he announced over dinner that he intended going
> on safari to Africa. While his mother laughed at the notion, Alex
> immediately set about gathering train and ship schedules, books
> about Africa, and iron bars for the cages that the Great White
> Hunter in their midst would need. Even his son admitted to being
> taken aback when Alex set a specific date for a departure, the plan
> being to catch a train to Baltimore for a connection to New York
> and, ultimately, the Atlantic. Everything was played out right to the
> final day, when Alex announced that the line to Baltimore had been
> blocked by a derailment and suggested a trip to Atlantic City, while
> waiting for the track to be cleared. It was only during the day in
> Atlantic City that James accepted his father's suggestion that maybe
> it would be better to wait a few years before undertaking the safari.
> That decision came as "a great relief."[14]

It takes an extraordinary father to create room under his authority,
within his paternity, for another to grow in freedom. It takes a
humble letting be, a Godly *gelassenheit,* because God who "lets be"
is the God revealed in the life and the death and the sacrament of
Jesus that we celebrate.

Captain Kangaroo

Where's that point in life when one stops growing up and starts
growing old? It's probably more a series than a single point. Certainly one such moment is the death of a childhood friend. How
melancholy, when a sense of loss mingles with a knowledge of
neglect. You realize that you haven't thought about your friend in
a long, long time. You feel bad about that, especially because your
guilt keeps being overwhelmed by wonderful childhood memories.

How did the press of adulthood squeeze out images of so much joy?

If you're between the ages of fifty-five and twenty-five, you could have empathized with my melancholy mood of joy and regret when I learned in January of 2004 that Bob Keeshan had died. I never knew that he was the original Clarabell the Clown on *The Puppet Playhouse*.[15] I didn't know that he was of Irish descent or that he lived in Babylon, Long Island, and caught the commuter train each morning at four thirty to be on time at the CBS studios. I didn't know that he did a live show for the East Coast and, an hour later, turned around and did the same for me in Kansas.[16] I only knew that he was my Captain Kangaroo.[17]

I certainly didn't know that he had turned down the suggestion of a live studio audience of children, insisting that he wanted the child at home to see him as there for him or her alone. That was certainly my Captain. Who would have read *Curious George* to me if he hadn't taken the time? And I knew that the Magic Drawing Board wasn't really magic, but I couldn't explain how those images appeared. I watched them as though they were conjuring the world out of nothing. I grew up around farms, but no farming uncle of mine ever held an animal on his knee, inviting me to take a closer look, the way the Captain's friend Mr. Green Jeans did. It's sad to think that Mr. Moose and Bunny no longer have a foil for their practical jokes. What will they do with those Ping-Pong balls now?

I'm sure my mother would be embarrassed to have me write that I can't remember if I had a birthday cake every year, but I do know that on the first day of every month the Captain would wheel out a cake for all the birthdays that month. My birthday is the first of June. I never missed the cake, and my favorite part was watching the time-lapse films of flowers opening while someone sang, "June is bustin' out all over."

Many Christians suffer from what I call "gospel glaucoma." We're too familiar with the stories to experience their luster. It's as though we're watching a movie where Jesus has been so obviously cast as the Messiah. We can't help but wonder why others are so slow on the take. We can't make the sympathetic leap that would allow us to enter the world of the Gospel. What would it mean for someone to stand up in our assembly and say, "The Spirit of the Lord is upon me, because he has anointed me to bring good news to the poor. He has sent me to proclaim release to the captives and recovery of sight to the blind, to let the oppressed go free, to proclaim the year of the Lord's favor" (Luke 4:18-19). Would we really believe the world to be a fundamentally different place simply because someone said it was?

We read the Gospel through the lenses of the death and resurrection. Of course Jesus is everything that he says he is. That's the whole point of the story whether it's true or not, right? And there's the rub. Two thousand years later, who can say? But two thousand years ago, real men and women listened to an ordinary man and felt their world begin to move. They began to see things they had never really seen. Something happened; some grace stirred and made the ordinary world a different place.

The same thing happened when a weary band of refugees finally made their way back to Jerusalem from Babylon and listened as Ezra the scribe read out the law they had been hearing their whole lives (Neh 8). Suddenly, back in a ruined city, their long-desired city, it could be heard again as though for the first time.

The question is not what it would take to make the story of Jesus true. That's a valid question, and I think it has a good answer. The bigger question is, what would it take to make the story matter? What would have to happen in our lives for us to really hear, to truly see? What wakes the human person from slumber? Death? Losing a job? Falling in love? Having a baby? Breaking a limb? Running out of gin? Losing an Internet or cable connection?

You see, before the world can be a magical place, a place of grace, it must first be an empty place. It needs to be drained of the dredge that darkens everyday life. Spiritual glaucoma is such a gradual, insidious affliction. So how does a stiffening adult suddenly stumble into a world of grace and wonder?

Somehow we have to find our way back to that point in life where the world was empty enough to make room for a man with a walrus mustache who came every morning at eight o'clock and suffused the world with wonder and delight: a dancing bear, a Magic Drawing Board, a farmer who had all the time in the world for animals and kids, and a captain with a terribly silly name and a task as old as the Gospel itself, because, in his own way, that was his task. "The Spirit of the Lord is upon me."

Uncle Bill

Heroes make it look easy. As a child watching them on television, I thought adulthood would be a snap. It would mean getting to do whatever I wanted, like eating chocolate-chip cookie dough before it's baked or having Jell-O pudding not *with* every meal but *for* every meal. My adult role models faced everything with perfect equanimity, doing what they had to do with seemingly endless resources.

But here I am at midlife with no chocolate-chip cookie dough, and I can't even remember when I last had Jell-O Pudding. Now, I can't help but wonder, how did Uncle Bill of *Family Affair* do it?[18] I wouldn't have known what to do with Buffy, much less Jody and Sissy! I do know that Mr. French would have had to shake up one heck of a martini before I remodeled my African Safari den into a child's bedroom!

Think of the boundless human resources our TV heroes had at their disposal. Aunt Bee always had a pie in the oven. Andy never angrily put Barney in his place. There was never any question but that Kate Bradley would raise Billie Jo, Betty Jo, and Bobby Jo with flawless maternal wisdom. If Steve Douglas couldn't be father and mother to his three sons, it didn't matter, because Uncle Charlie was there. As far as I could see, the only real challenge to being an adult would be the possibility that you might find a kooky genie in a bottle or accidently end up with Endora the Witch as your mother-in-law. The Professor and Gilligan were young men who had no problem living in balmy straw huts next to the voluptuous Ginger and the openly midriff-baring Mary Ann. That didn't seem like such an accomplishment at the time, but now I wonder about the Professor and Gilligan!

How do real adults manage to avoid being a Gladys Kravitz or a Mrs. Drysdale? How do they rise above the greed of a Mr. Haney, when life really is short and not all that fair? How do they find the strength to go to work each day when they don't have a great job writing jokes with Sally and Murray? What if you don't have Laura in those cute, black Capri pants to come home to?

The Beverly Hills, the Park Avenue, even the German prisoner-of-war camp that I knew on television as a child were graced places. Everything always worked out for the best in Hooterville and Mayberry.

I'm not Uncle Bill or Kate Bradley or Stephen Douglas. I don't have the wisdom of Patty's dad or Lou Grant. I do believe that we can only be human when we reach beyond the human, when we believe that the script we've been given plays itself out on a stage beyond this life. "Then he looked up at his disciples and said: 'Blessed are you who are poor, for yours is the kingdom of God. Blessed are you who are hungry now, for you will be filled. Blessed are you who weep now, for you will laugh'" (Luke 6:20-21). One can certainly argue that the Beatitudes, and religion itself, by preaching a world beyond this one, keep us from being fully engaged in the struggle we call the real world.

But there's the paradox! So many of those who have been most effective in changing this world carried within them the conviction that what we see around us isn't all there is, that we are ordered to something beyond ourselves, that every human value has to be reevaluated in the light of a power, a beauty, and a truth that surpasses all human values. It's hard to run without looking ahead, hard to leap up without picturing one's self as going much higher in the sky than we actually do.

Television seemed to come with grace included. No matter how much Lucy messed up, Ricky would still love her. Gilligan might foil a hundred rescue efforts, but no one would ever vote him off the island. Real life isn't like that. Or is it? Somehow believing that it is seems to make all the difference. Join us again, next week, to find out.

Notes

Preview, pages vii–x

1. *The Patty Duke Show,* 30 min., ABC, 1963–66.

2. *Universal Catechism of the Catholic Church,* 2nd ed. (New York: Doubleday, 2003), pars. 1024–25.

3. Jean-Paul Sartre, *No Exit,* In *No Exit and Three Other Plays* (New York: Vintage International, 1989), 45.

Chapter 1, pages 1–17

1. Ignatius of Loyola, *The Spiritual Exercises,* in *Ignatius of Loyola: The Spiritual Exercises and Selected Works,* ed. George E. Ganss (New York: Paulist Press, 1991), 201.

2. *Adventures of Superman,* 30 min., MPTV, 1952–58.

3. See the *Universal Catechism of the Catholic Church,* par. 43.

4. *De veritate* q. 2, a.1, co.

5. Paul Tillich, "Waiting," in *The Shaking of the Foundations* (New York: Charles Scribner's Sons, 1948), 149–51.

6. William Frye, "The Wizard of Roz," *Vanity Fair* 500 (April 2002): 278–85, at 282.

7. Ibid., 285.

8. Stefan Kanfer, *Ball of Fire: The Tumultuous Life and Comic Art of Lucille Ball* (New York: Alfred Knopf, 2003), 12–13.

9. Ibid., 16.

10. *Days of Our Lives,* 30 min. (1965–75); 60 min. (1975–), Corday Productions.

11. *The Westminster Collection of Christian Prayers,* ed. Dorothy M. Stewart (Louisville, KY: John Knox Press, 2002), 126.

12. Augustine, *The Confessions,* trans. Maria Boulding, ed. John E. Rotelle. Vol. I/1, *The Works of St. Augustine: A Translation for the 21st Century* (Hyde Park, New York: New City Press, 1997), 262 (X, 27).

13. Monica Furlong, *Visions and Longings: Medieval Women Mystics* (Boston: Shambhala, 1996), 114.

Chapter 2, pages 18–38

1. *Roman Holiday,* 118 min., Paramount Pictures, 1953.

2. *My Fair Lady,* 170 min., Warner Bros. Pictures, 1964.

3. *Sabrina,* 113 min., Paramount Pictures, 1954.

4. *Breakfast at Tiffany's,* 115 min., Jurow-Shepherd, 1961.

5. *The Nun's Story,* 149 min., Warner Bros. Pictures, 1959.

6. Stefan Kanfer, *Ball of Fire: The Tumultuous Life and Comic Art of Lucille Ball* (New York: Alfred Knopf, 2003), 131–32.

7. Ibid., 146.

8. *Universal Catechism of the Catholic Church,* 2nd ed. (New York: Doubleday, 2003), par. 1996.

9. Gerard Manley Hopkins, *The Poetical Works of Gerard Manley Hopkins,* ed. Norman H. Mackenzie (Oxford: Clarendon Press, 1992), 139.

10. J. R. R. Tolkien, "On Fairy Stories," in *The Monsters and the Critics and Other Essays,* ed. Christopher Tolkien (Boston: Houghton Mifflin, 1983), 147. Those interested in pursuing the Christian foundations of Tolkien's fantasy would undoubtedly enjoy Bradley Birzer's J. R. R. *Tolkien's Sanctifying Myth: Understanding Middle-Earth* (Wilmington, DE: ISI Books, 2003).

11. J. R. R. Tolkien, "On Fairy Stories," 153.

12. Humphrey Carpenter, ed., *The Letters of J. R. R. Tolkien* (Boston: Houghton Mifflin, 1981), 172.

13. C. S. Lewis, "Myth Became Fact," in *God in the Dock: Essays on Theology and Ethics,* ed. Walter Hooper (Grand Rapids, MI: Eerdmans, 1970), 66.

14. J. R. R. Tolkien, "On Fairy Stories," 156.

15. Humphrey Carpenter, ed. *The Letters of J. R. R. Tolkien,* 274–75.

16. J. R. R. Tolkien, *The Return of the King* (Boston: Houghton Mifflin Company, 1965), 213.

17. Tina Brown, *The Diana Chronicles* (New York: Doubleday, 2007), 175.

18. Joseph Ratzinger, *Jesus of Nazareth,* trans. Adrian J. Walker (New York: Doubleday, 2007), 76.

19. Cary Grant, "Archie Leach," *Ladies Home Journal* 80, no. 1 (Jan–Feb 1963): 50–53, 133–42, at 133. The autobiographical piece was serialized and also appears in the March and April issues.

20. Jean-Luc Marion, *God without Being Hors-Text,* trans. by Thomas A. Carlson (Chicago: The University of Chicago Press, 1991), 169.

21. Ibid., 177.

22. Grant, "Archie Leach," 134.

23. Donald Spoto, *Enchantment: The Life of Audrey Hepburn* (New York: Harmony Books, 2006), 28.

Chapter 3, pages 39–53

1. *The Sound of Music,* 174 min., Robert Wise Productions, 1965.

2. *Leave It to Beaver,* 30 min., American Broadcasting Company, 1957–63.

3. *My Favorite Martian,* 30 min., CBS Television, 1963–66.

4. Augustine, *De Trinitate,* VIII–IX.

5. *Gone with the Wind,* 226 min., Selznick International Pictures, 1939.

6. Claudia Roth Pierpont, "Born for the Part," *New Yorker,* July 14, 2003, 52–63, at 58.

7. Ibid., 58.

8. Ibid., 63.

9. John of the Cross, "The Dark Night," in *The Collected Works of St. John of the Cross* (Washington: ICS Publications, 1979), 294–389, at 359.

10. Claudia Roth Pierpont, "Born for the Part," 63.

11. Annie Proulx, "Brokeback Mountain," *New Yorker,* October 13, 1997, 74–85.

12. Ibid., 85.

13. Joseph Ratzinger, "The Beauty and Truth of Christ," *L'Osservatore Romano* (English edition), November 6, 2002, 6.

14. Ibid.

15. Bob Colacello, "Ronnie and Nancy," *Vanity Fair* 528 (August 2004): 158–65, 220–26, at 221.

16. Ibid., 221.

17. Ibid.

18. Augustine, *The Confessions, The Works of St. Augustine: A Translation for the 21st Century,* vol. I/1, trans. Maria Boulding, ed. John E. Rotelle (Hyde Park, New York: New City Press, 1997), 75 (III.1).

19. Augustine, *Sermons, The Works of St. Augustine: A Translation for the 21st Century,* vol. III/2, 166 (XXXIV).

20. Augustine, *The Confessions,* 263 (X.29).

21. Bob Colacello, "Ronnie and Nancy," 162.

22. Ibid., 226.

Chapter 4, pages 54–70

1. Frank DiGiacomo, "A Rock of Her Own," *Vanity Fair* 552 (August 2006): 144–150, 188–191.

2. Ibid., 188.

3. Ibid., 189.

4. Ibid.

5. Ibid., 190.

6. Ibid., 189.

7. Ibid., 146.

8. Ibid., 189.

9. Donald Spoto, *Enchantment: The Life of Audrey Hepburn* (New York: Harmony Books, 2006), 4.

10. Ibid., 11–12.

11. Ibid., 228.

12. Ibid., 73–74.

13. Michel de Certeau, "How Is Christianity Thinkable Today?" in *The Postmodern God: A Theological Reader,* ed. Graham Ward, 142–55 (Malden, MA: Blackwell, 1997), 145.

14. Spoto, *Enchantment,* 146.

15. Ibid.

16. Leslie Bennetts, "The Unsinkable Jennifer Aniston," *Vanity Fair* 541 (September 2005): 331–39, 390–94.

17. Ibid., 391.

18. Ibid.

19. Robert Gottlieb, "DAH-LING: The Strange Case of Tallulah Bankhead," *New Yorker* (May 16, 2005): 82.

20. Ibid.

21. Ibid.

22. Ibid., 84.

23. Ibid.

24. Ibid., 86.

25. Ibid.

Chapter 5, pages 71–91

1. Stefan Kanfer, *Ball of Fire: The Tumultuous Life and Comic Art of Lucille Ball* (New York: Alfred Knopf, 2003), 207.

2. Ibid., 225.

3. *The Sopranos,* 58 min., Home Box Office, 1999–2007.

4. Charles McGrath, "Ending without Endings," *New York Times,* June 17, 2007, Late Edition–Final, sec. 4; col. 4; Week in Review Desk; IDEAS & TRENDS; 14.

5. Dan Brown, *The Da Vinci Code* (New York: Doubleday, 2003), 231–34.

6. Ibid., 231.

7. Alexandra Stanley, "Wearied by Reality, Television Returns To a 1980's Mind-Set," *New York Times,* July 24, 2002, Late Edition (East Coast), E1.

8. *I Dream of Jeannie,* 30 min., National Broadcasting Company (NBC), 1965–70.

9. *De Veritate* 1,1.

10. Scholars are in agreement that chapter 20 represents the original ending of St. John's Gospel. Chapter 21 is an addendum.

Chapter 6, pages 92–113

1. J. K. Rowling, *Harry Potter and the Sorcerer's Stone* (New York: Arthur A. Levine Books, 1997), 50–51.

2. Ibid., 51.

3. *Universal Catechism of the Catholic Church,* 2nd ed. (New York: Doubleday, 2003), par. 2558.

4. *Gilligan's Island,* 30 min., CBS Television, 1964–67.

5. St. John of the Cross, "The Ascent of Mount Carmel," in *The Collected Works of St. John of the Cross,* 66–292 (Washington: ICS Publications, 1979), 243.

6. Søren Kierkegaard, *Purity of Heart is to Will One Thing: Spiritual Preparation for the Office of Confession* (New York: Harper, 1956).

7. *Green Acres,* 30 min., CBS Television, 1965–71.

8. *Star Trek,* 47 min., Desilu Productions, 1966–69.

9. *Enterprise,* 42 min., Braga Productions, 2001–2005.

10. Donald Dewey, *James Stewart: A Biography* (Atlanta: Turner Publishing, Inc., 1996), 11.

11. Ibid., 54–55.

12. Ibid., 55.

13. Ibid., 60.

14. Ibid., 60–61.

15. *The Puppet Playhouse,* 30 min., NBC, 1947–60.

16. Richard Severo, "Bob Keeshan, Creator and Star of TV's 'Captain Kangaroo' is Dead at 76," *New York Times,* January 24, 2004, A13.

17. *Captain Kangaroo,* 30 min., Robert Keeshan Associates, 1955–92.

18. *Family Affair,* 30 min., CBS, 1966–71.